The Sounds of English
VOWELS

Key Words	Webster's Diacritical Markings	Funk & Wagnalls' Markings Key 1	International Phonetic Alphabet
eagle	ē	ī	iː
city	ĭ	i	ɪ
senate	å	ı	ɪт
elephant	ĕ	e	eт
airplane	â	ā	ɛː
apple	ă	a	æ
dance	ȧ	ʁ	ɐ
world	û	ū̄	ɜː
abroad	ă		
also ȧ—sofa			
ĕ—recent			
ŏ—connect	ə	ə
ŭ—circus			
ẽr—maker			
umbrella	ŭ	ᴜ	ʌ
tools	ōō	ū	uː
football	ŏŏ	u	ᴜ
obey	ō	o	oт
automobile	ô	ō̄	ɔː
golf	ǒ	ɵ	ɒ
garden	ä	ɑ	ɑː

Diphthongs

fable	ā	ē	eɪ̆
knight	ī	ai	aɪ̆
ocean	ō	ō	oᴜ̆
cowboy	ou	au	ɑᴜ
oil	oi	ɵi	ɔɪ̆
ear	ẽr	īr	ɪə̆
hair	âr	ār	ɛə
poor	ōōr	ūr	ᴜə̆
four	ōr	ōr	ɔə̆
unite	û	iu	juː

IMPROVING YOUR SPEECH

A Pupil's Practice Book in Speech Training

WITH PHONETIC AIDS

BY

LETITIA RAUBICHECK, PH.D.

Director of Speech Improvement
New York City Public Schools

ILLUSTRATED BY

CHARLES W. RAUBICHECK

NOBLE AND NOBLE, *Publishers, Inc.*
100 FIFTH AVENUE - - - NEW YORK CITY

Preface for the Teacher

During the past decade, paralleling the growth of the radio broadcast and the talking motion picture, there has been an ever-growing interest in good speech. High schools and colleges have adopted courses in speech training, but they have realized that speech training must be begun in the elementary schools if it is to be really effective.

This book, therefore, is a pioneer in speech training for the intermediate grades of the elementary schools. It is based on sound pedagogical principles of beginning with the sound and expanding the lesson through words and phrases until the pupils can easily master the complete sentences. The entire book is arranged on the Unit Plan with a picture to motivate the lesson. Each unit represents a single sound. By the time the pupil has finished the book, he will have had practice in every sound of the English language.

This book may be used by pupils who have been taught by the phonic method, with its diacritical markings, or by the newer phonetic method using the international phonetic symbols. At the front of the book will be found a key for transposing one system to the other.

Diagnostic Tests

Before the class begins to study this book, each pupil should be asked to read aloud Diagnostic Tests I and II. The teacher should check each pupil's pronunciation of the key words found on pages 14 and 15. From a perfect score of 100 per cent, 5 points should be deducted for every mispronunciation. These scores should be kept on file for a final achievement test at the end of the term so that improvement may be noted. Perhaps the individual pupil may need practice on only a few particular sounds. In such cases the teacher could assign special drill on such sounds.

How to Use This Book

Different teachers will use this book in different ways, depending upon the type of child in the class. One way would be to take each unit in its regular order. This book is arranged with the simpler sounds first and progresses through the consonants to the more difficult vowels and diphthongs.

Build the lesson around the picture. Be sure that all the pupils can pronounce the sound correctly. Let them discuss the picture and make up simple oral compositions about what they see.

Then proceed to the words. Group I contains the simpler words, but most children will have no difficulty in understanding the meaning of the more advanced words in Group II.

When every pupil has had an opportunity to pronounce the words, the class may proceed to the phrases and later to the sentences.

In answering the questions at the end of each unit, try to have each pupil reply with a sentence containing as many words as possible that illustrate the sound being studied.

The practice afforded by this book should greatly improve the oral English in other subjects. Good speech should become a habit, for it is the mark of every educated person.

Additional suggestions for the teaching of Speech will be found in Raubicheck's *How to Teach Good Speech in the Elementary Schools*, Noble and Noble, Publishers, Inc., New York.

Acknowledgments

The Author wishes to make the following acknowledgments—to Superintendent John J. Loftus for his generous assistance in valuable revisions of the manuscript; to Superintendent Oswald Schlockow, pioneer in the movement for scientific speech training, for his liberal encouragement and thoughtful suggestions; to Superintendent Anna A. Short for her interest and cooperation; to Superintendent Charles E. O'Neill, under whose inspiration and guidance have been developed a most comprehensive and progressive speech program; to Miss Jeanette Molloy for her many helpful criticisms.

Contents

PHONETIC AIDS

A Story About Speech

Once upon a time two countries were at war with each other. The king of one ancient land decreed that if any stranger came to the entrance of the country and asked to come in, the guards should say to him, "Are you a stranger?"

If he said, "No, I'm a native. I belong here," then the king told the guards that they should test him.

They should ask him to pronounce one word. If he said it correctly, they were to let him enter. If, however, he mispronounced this word, they would know that he was not a native and they should put him to death.

That word was "Shibboleth." If he belonged to the country, he said it "Shibboleth" and was saved. If he pronounced it "Sibboleth," they knew he was an enemy and they killed him!

Nowadays, of course, we don't kill people because of the way they pronounce words, but it is still possible to tell a great many things about a person just by hearing him speak.

We, too, have our "Shibboleths." You will find some of them on page 137.

Where We Need Good Speech

Have you any idea how many times you speak during the day? This morning when your mother called you to get up for school you probably spoke to her. Did you have to ask your mother where your stockings or your clean blouse were? Did you say "Good morning" when you sat down to the table to eat your breakfast?

Did you meet any of your friends on the way to school? What did you do when you saw them? What happened when you came into the classroom? Did you speak to anyone? How many people have you spoken to since you left home this morning? It would be fun to keep a list of all the people to whom you speak.

Why We Need Good Speech

We are using speech all the time—at work, in school, at play in the street, while we are at home, when we go to parties. If we speak so that people can understand what we say, and if our voices are pleasant to listen to, people will enjoy listening to us more than if we mumble or speak in an unpleasant manner. This book will help you to speak well and to have fun while you are learning.

How We May Learn to Speak Well

First we must learn to listen to the way we speak and the way other people speak to us. Then we can decide which way we like best. Next we shall study the machine which we use in speaking. After that we shall study the sounds of our language and how each one is made. Lastly, we shall practice using these sounds in speech.

3

The Speech Machine

Let us get acquainted with the organs we use in speaking. A small mirror will be a great help to you. Perhaps your mother has one in an old handbag, which she would give you. Hold the mirror in your right hand and put your left hand under your right elbow. Now hold the mirror opposite your mouth, so that you can see it without bending over.

How far out can you stretch your tongue? Can you touch your nose with it? Can you reach the point of your chin with it? Can you make a point on the end of your tongue? Your tongue must be very nimble if you are going to speak well, so we shall give it plenty of exercise.

You see that for the sound of [t] as in "tea," for instance, the tip of the tongue is used. For [k] as in "cake" the back of the tongue is used. For [j] as in "yes" the middle of the tongue is used.

What part of the tongue is used for [n] as in "noon"?

Now let us see what we can do with our lips. Can you push out your lips until they make a small circle? This is the position for [uː] as in "zoo."

Now can you stretch the lips into a wide grin, showing all your upper front teeth? This is the position for [iː] as in "see."

Some of the sounds are made with the aid of the front teeth. For instance, make the sound of [f] as in "fire." Notice where the teeth and lips are placed.

Now put the finger-tips of your right hand on your throat, just where a man's Adam's apple is. Make the sound of [ɑː] as in "palm." Do you feel a slight buzzing under your finger-tips? That is made by the voice. The Adam's

4

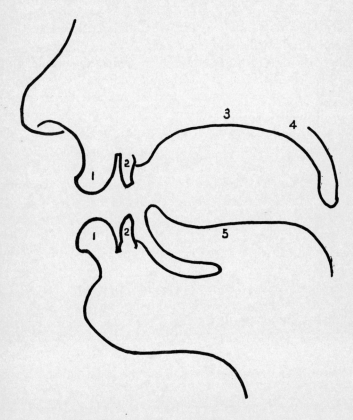

1. The lips   3. The hard palate

2. The teeth   4. The soft palate

5. The tongue

apple is the voice box or larynx, and all our voice is made right there. Two little strings like rubber bands are stretched across the opening of the voice box. They are like the strings of a violin. These strings are called "vocal cords." When we want to make a voiced sound, we send the breath out against these little strings and they vibrate or buzz. This is what makes the sound of voice which we hear.

Now put your right hand on the bridge of your nose and say, "Ding, dong, bell," holding on to the last sound of each word. Do you feel another buzzing up in your nose? That means that the sound which is made in the larynx or voice box is being made louder up in your nose, just as a loud speaker in a radio makes the sound louder. We also have "amplifiers" in our mouths and in our throats, and if we use them well we can speak loudly enough to be heard without screaming. We will also have pleasant voices if we use these "loud speakers" in the right way.

Daily Drill for Good Speech

Here are a set of exercises which will keep the voice machine in good condition and make good speech possible. Hold your mirror in position to help you to do these exercises well. Repeat each exercise three times.

1. Stretch the tip of your tongue out and down as far as you can toward the point of your chin. Ready: out and down, in.
2. Stretch the tip of your tongue up towards the tip of your nose. Ready: out and up, in.
3. Now do first exercise one, then exercise two. Ready: out and down, in; out and up, in.
4. Raise the tip of your tongue to the roof of your mouth just behind the upper front teeth. Now bulge your tongue out so that the under side of it shows. Ready: lift, bulge, rest.
5. Now place the tip of your tongue behind your lower front teeth and bulge it out until the middle of the upper surface of your tongue shows. Ready: lower, bulge, rest.
6. Now do first Exercise 4 and then Exercise 5 like this. Ready: lift, bulge, rest; lower, bulge, rest.
7. Place the tip of the tongue so that it touches the lower front teeth. Raise the back of the tongue towards the roof of the mouth. Ready: raise, lower, rest.
8. Now raise the tip of the tongue to the roof of the mouth as though you were saying n. Lower it and raise the back of the tongue to the roof of the mouth as though you were saying g. Ready: raise tip up; rest; back of the tongue up; rest.

9. Now swing the tongue around the lips beginning at the right. Open your mouth and lick the lips as if there were chocolate icing on them. Ready: tongue in the right-hand corner of the mouth, up, around, down, in.

10. Repeat Exercise 9, beginning at the left-hand corner of the mouth. Ready: left, up, around, down, in.

11. Now swing the tongue around the lips, first from the right and then from the left. Ready: right, around, down, in; left, around, down, in.

12. Now make a groove in the middle of your tongue by raising the sides and folding them over towards the center. Blow through this groove. Ready: fold, blow, rest.

Do these exercises every day and you will be able to speak clearly without too much effort.

How Well Do You Hear?

1. Do you know these sounds when you hear them?

    an automobile horn   riveting
    a factory whistle   your front door closing
    a church bell   your father's footsteps
    brakes screeching   your dog's bark

2. Can you tell the difference between

    an automobile horn and a fog horn;
    an ambulance siren and that on a policeman's motorcycle;
    a scissors grinder and an old-clothes man;
    a radio and a hurdy-gurdy?

3. What kind of sound do these make?

    a peanut stand   a rooster   a dog
    a cow   a cat   a canary

4. How many radio programs can you recognize even if you do not know the station nor hear the announcement?

5. How many radio stars have lovely voices? How many sound silly because of the voice quality which they use? Which voice do you like best on the air? Which do you dislike most? Can you tell what makes one attractive and the other unpleasant?

6. Can you read this sentence as if you were

    a little old lady   a pleasant lady or gentleman
    a very rude boy   a cross little girl

    "Where are you going?"

Daily Drill for Good Voice

All voice is made on the out-going breath. In order to have controlled voices we must first have controlled breath. Let us see how much control we really have. Take in a quiet breath and then let it out with a tiny hiss, like a leak in a radiator. How long can you keep that tiny hiss going? Is it steady or does it come out in spurts? Can you make it steady by trying?

Now place your hands on your waist-line in front and cough gently. What action do you feel beneath your hands? That contraction of the muscles forces the air out of your lungs, up your wind pipe, over your voice box and through your nose and mouth. When you shout, "Stop," the same thing happens. Try calling aloud, "Halt," "Fire," "Oh," with a contraction of the muscles under your hands. This time, instead of shouting quickly, press steadily and quietly against those muscles and press out the words, "Arms," "We," "Who."

Let us try in each of these exercises to feel that steady pressing out as we make voice.

1. Take in a quiet breath around the waist and count slowly in a whisper—one, two, three, four.
2. Take in a quiet breath around the waist and count aloud slowly—one, two, three, four.
3. Whisper—one, two, three, four, five, six.
4. Count aloud—one, two, three, four, five, six.
5. Whisper the alphabet as far as "h," then on the next breath as far as "o." Finally, finish the alphabet with the next breath. Do not hurry.

6. Repeat the alphabet aloud, dividing it as you did in Exercise 5.

7. First whisper the following sounds, taking a quiet breath between each one and pressing out steadily. Then say them aloud in the same way.

ah, ay, ee, aw, oh, oo.

8. Whisper these syllables in the same way. Pause for breath wherever you see this sign /. Then say them aloud in the same way.

tah, tay, tee, taw, toh, too/ kah, kay, kee, kaw, koh, koo/ quah, quay, quee, quaw, quoh, quoo/.

9. Whisper these words, pressing out steadily. Then say them aloud in the same way.

see, sit, set, fair, fat, fast/ firm, supper/ pool, put, pole, Paul, pond, palm.

10. Now say aloud the sounds underlined in the words used in Exercise 9.

11. Whisper these sentences and then say them aloud.

She is getting there at last.
Serve the lunch.
You would go call on Martha.

12. Make these sounds ring in your nose.

sing, sang, song.   ding, dang, dong.   ling, lang, long.
ring, rang, rong.   bing, bang, bong.   kling, klang, klong.

11

Diagnostic Test I—Form A[1]

Sounds Frequently Mispronounced:

Diacritical Marks: ă, z, ou, ô, ng, th, r, oi, ir, ĭ, th, ng;
t, s, d.

Phonetic Symbols: æ, z, aʊ, ɔː, ŋ, θ, ɹ, ɔɪ, ɜː, aɪ, đ, ŋg,
t, s, d.

SPRING BEAUTY

The apple trees are in bloom now. All the birds
are singing in the branches. The thrush and the
robin are building nests in the oak tree. Girls and
boys join in gathering up the old leaves and burning
them. Our dog is running around and barking
eagerly. We find violets under the tangled dead
leaves. They are just tight buds now, but will
soon open in the hot sun.

Did you ever try to find violets in the spring?

---

[1] For directions in administering and rating these tests, see page iii in the
Preface.

Diagnostic Test II

Double Consonants:

Initial: fl, bl, cr, gr, sm, cl, tr, pr, br, sk, sp, pl, sl, fr, gl.

Medial: tl, nd

Final: st, sk, ts

SPORT ON SPRING DAYS

The flowers that bloom in the spring are lovely. The shy violets creep out from the grass. Small boys climb high up in the peach trees to pull down the pretty blossoms. Then they bring down their roller skates from the attic. Baseball and other outdoor sports now begin. The girls' play is more gentle but they have just as much fun. They play house under the trees. The children ask for more dessert at supper time and eat the last piece of cake.

After a hard day of playing in the fresh air, they are glad to go to bed early. They sleep well on these nights in spring.

Rating Sheet for Test I — Form A

Sounds Frequently Mispronounced:

Diacritical Marks: ă, z, ou, ô, ng, th, r, oi, ir, ī, th,
ŋg, t, s, d

Phonetic Symbols: æ, z, ɑʊ, ɔː, ŋ, θ, ɹ, ɔɪ, ɜː, aɪ, ð, ŋg,
t, s, d.

1. apple
2. trees
3. now
4. all
5. singing
6. thrush
7. robin
8. join

9. burning
10. find
11. under the
12. tangled
13. tight
14. soon
15. did

14

Rating Sheet for Test II

Double Consonants:

Initial: fl, bl, cr, gr, sm, cl, tr, pr, br, sk, sp, pl, fr, gl, sl

Medial: tl, nd

Final: st, sk, ts

1. flowers
2. bloom
3. creep
4. grass
5. small
6. climb
7. trees
8. pretty
9. bring
10. skates

11. sports
12. play
13. gentle
14. just
15. under
16. ask
17. fresh
18. glad
19. sleep
20. nights

The Sounds
of
English

I. Consonants

p is the first sound in "puppy." Press your lips lightly together. Now blow them apart with your breath. There are two ways of saying this sound. You can find out more about that on page 148.

Say these words aloud, listening for the sound of p.

Group I	Group II
peace	paper
pack	promise
pool	pepper
palm	happy
pane	appear
help	proud
sweep	print
slip	plump
hop	sponge
lamp	spring

Repeat each of these phrases three times.

pumpkin pie   plum pudding   pretty picture
pretty polly   plenty of pluck   pump it up
pots and pans   potatoes and peas   step up

18

In these sentences find the words which contain the sound
p.   *Then read the sentence aloud.*

1. Picking peaches is pleasant work.
2. Plums and pears grow in many places.
3. Help Peter to put his playthings away.
4. Hop, skip, and jump to bed.
5. Playing policeman is a popular game.
6. Pepper pot is the name of a good soup.
7. Polite people say, "Pardon me," when they pass in front of others.
8. Spice is used in making pickles and preserves.
9. Partridges are usually plump.
10. An I. O. U. is a promise to pay.

Can you answer these questions?   Try to use a word that contains the sound.

1. What kind of puppy would you like to own?
2. Which pupil in this class is the best speller?
3. What parks in America do you know?
4. What vegetable is dug out of the ground?
5. What three fruits grow on trees?

On page 28 you will find some more sentences containing this sound.

19

b is the first and fifth sound in "baseball." Press your lips lightly together as you did for p. This time blow them apart with the voiced breath.

Say these words aloud, listening for the sound of b.

Group I	Group II
tub	habit
rub	table
cab	bubble
mob	rubber
rib	tumble
book	trouble
butter	shrub
basket	cupboard
beef	suburb
bank	ramble

Repeat each of these phrases three times.

bounce the ball	a bunch of bananas	bacon and beans
brown bread	books for boys	bats and balls
the best butter	baby brother	blowing bubbles

In these sentences find the words which contain the sound of
b. *Then read the sentences aloud.*

1. The boy buys a bean bag.
2. Bobby's big brother brought him a rubber ball and a bat.
3. Put the beef and the beets in the basket.
4. Betty became a member of a sewing club.
5. The boys went crabbing in the row boat.
6. Mother bakes bran muffins for father and ginger-bread for Bill.
7. Spot, Bob's terrier, barks at the butcher boy.
8. Buffalo Bill was a cowboy.
9. Beatrice spread the peanut butter on the bread.
10. A branch of the beech tree was broken by the wind.

Can you answer these questions?

1. In what state is Boston?
2. Where is the Bay of Biscay?
3. Have you a big brother?
4. What does a Boy Scout badge look like?
5. How is butter made?

You will find some more practice sentences on page 28.

21

m is the first sound in "mail."　Close your lips and make a voiced sound through your nose.

Say these words aloud, listening for the sound of m.

Group I	*Group II*
meadow	hammer
mark	somebody
middle	humming
mouse	promise
meal	promote
music	fumble
drum	chimney
flame	lumber
plum	company
slam	coming
blossom	swim
lamb	chum

Repeat each of these phrases three times.

mountains move　　merry men of Gotham
more and more　　murmuring and mumbling
making merry　　humming in the middle of the morning

In these sentences find the words that contain the sound of **m.**
Then read the sentences aloud.

1. Men make machines to make work easy.
2. The members of the team were covered with mud.
3. The man with the ball fumbled.
4. Mother and Mary made muffins for tea.
5. Mary's lamb was very tame.
6. Come and have some plum cake.
7. Marion thought it jolly to sit in the rumble seat.
8. Martin promised to climb trees with his chum, Jim.
9. Someone smelled smoke and sent for the firemen.
10. The scouts marched with the fife and drum.

Can you answer these questions?

1. Can you recite one stanza of a memory gem?
2. How many summer sports can you name?
3. Are monkeys as afraid of mice as elephants are?
4. How far can you swim?
5. Do lumbermen live in camps?

If you need more practice on this sound turn to page 28.

ᴡʜ is the first sound in "whale." Push out your lips and make a small circle. Now blow through the little opening.

Say these words aloud, listening for the sound of ᴡ.

Group I	*Group II*
what	anywhere
whether	whitewash
wheat	elsewhere
whistle	somewhere
whittle	whenever
which	whippoorwill
wheel	whirl
whisper	whisk
whiskers	whine
whip	white

Repeat each of these phrases three times.

the whip whistles	where is the white one
whittle wood	one whisper
whippoorwill	what a way
which way is west	which wave

In these sentences find the words which begin with ᴍ. *Then read the sentences aloud.*

1. Whenever I whistle, my dog barks.
2. Where does the sun rise in winter?
3. The whippoorwill whistles in the summer twilight.
4. Which way will you go?
5. Whales have fins with which they guide themselves while swimming.
6. The wind whistled through the wheat.
7. Straws show which way the wind blows.
8. Moby Dick was a white whale.
9. Four white mice with long white whiskers were whetting their teeth on the wooden stick.
10. Whether it rain or whether it snow, we shall have weather, whether or no.

Exercise for w *and* ᴍ. *Say aloud:*

not wear *but* where   *not* witch *but* which
not wen *but* when   *not* wy *but* why
            not watt *but* what

On page 28 find the sentences which contain words beginning with ᴍ.

w is the first sound in "wind." Push out your lips as you did for ᴍ. Blow a voiced sound through the small opening.

Say these words aloud, listening for the sound of w.

Group I	Group II
weeds	brickwork
witch	beware
weather	banquet
woods	roadway
sway	runaway
swim	swarm
dwell	swallow
quick	swing
queen	swagger
question	swamp

Repeat each of these phrases three times.

watch the work   weary with walking
one way walk   weather wise
warm weather   women of the western world

26

In these sentences find the words which contain the sound w. *Then read the sentences aloud.*

1. Witches walk on Hallowe'en.
2. Two men are on watch when the weather is rough at sea.
3. Once wonderful jewels were found in Mexico.
4. The homes of the cliff dwellers are found in the West.
5. Twenty cities were captured during the war.
6. Winifred went away without waiting for her friends.
7. Walter wore a silver watch.
8. One way of winning is to wish on the wishing stone.
9. I do not like winter weather because of the wind and the rain.
10. Queen Wilhelmina of Holland is one of the few women who are queens in their own right.

Can you answer these questions?

1. When was the western trail to Oregon discovered?
2. With what Indian tribe did William Penn make peace?
3. Can you name twelve cities west of the Mississippi?
4. Can swallows swim?
5. What two waterways lead through Canada to the ocean?

On page 28 you will find some more sentences containing this sound.

Review of the Lip Consonants

p, b, m, ʍ, w

1. Pike's Peak is the highest point in the Rocky Mountains.
2. The hippopotamus is not a playful animal.
3. Are sponges animals, vegetables, or minerals?
4. The big boys built bookcases in the workshop.
5. William made a sailboat out of pitch pine.
6. The boats in the harbor were blowing their horns.
7. Bruce had a black and blue spot on his back.
8. Peach blossoms are pink and white.
9. Peter tumbled off the limb of the apple tree.
10. Martin did a lot of damage with a hammer.
11. Do you ever wonder where the sun hides at night?
12. Whatever you do, do it with a will.
13. Climbing mountains is a fine summer sport.
14. How can you tell which way the wind is blowing?
15. Many pretty pictures are made by the frost on the window pane.
16. Wind and weather wear out a boat.
17. Bernard's black and white puppy won a prize at the dog show.
18. "The Prince and the Pauper" is the name of a fine story.
19. Polly made a bread and butter pudding.
20. Ben built a bonfire out of paper boxes.
21. Mary and Martha picked up pebbles on the beach.
22. Mother waited for Walter to bring some buns home from the baker's.
23. Which way shall we walk?
24. Bobby bounced his rubber ball against the wall.

25. The brothers played baseball in the park.
26. Commodore Perry commanded a brig in the Battle of Lake Erie.
27. Peter put his pride in his pocket and apologized to Pauline.
28. What makes the waves so high today?
29. Boys wear white flannels in summer.
30. Pink poppies look pretty in a blue bowl.
31. Ben belongs to the basketball team.
32. William was chosen to speak in the assembly.
33. When Walter Scott was a boy, he was interested in the Border Ballads.
34. Some camps begin the day with a bugle call.
35. Boys play football in the autumn.   What do they play in the spring?
36. Peru and Brazil are both members of the Pan-American League.
37. Baked beans and apple pie are American dishes.
38. Boys spin tops while girls jump rope.
39. Some western farmers use tractors instead of plows.
40. An ancient warrior bade his men beat their swords into plowshares.   Do you know what he meant?
41. One of the bloodiest battles of the Civil War was fought at Gettysburg.
42. Big brown birds with white wings swept through the air.
43. The policeman blew his whistle while Patrick brought his Pontiac to the curb.
44. "When the swallows homeward fly" is an old song.
45. "Oh, East is East and West is West
    And never the twain shall meet."

f is the first sound in "fish." Bite your lower lip lightly with your upper teeth and blow out.

Say these words aloud, listening for the sound of f.

Group I	Group II
fancy	offer
feed	affect
fit	defend
fern	affair
food	offend
laugh	enough
free	stuff
flag	staff
fresh	refresh
frost	flight

Repeat each of these phrases three times.

fair and free	fine feathers	friendly faces
fancy flying	French fans	fresh fish
fear or favor	fashionable folks	fiercely frowning

30

In these sentences find the words which contain the sound of f. *Then read the sentences aloud.*

1. Few French people settled in the South.
2. Polite people fear to offend their friends by speaking too frankly.
3. Feverfew is the name of a flower.
4. The frog frightened Florence by jumping from the side of the pond.
5. Frances found a four-leaved clover.
6. The baker left a loaf of fresh bread.
7. The flowers were reflected in the mirror.
8. Flora's face was reflected in the fountain.
9. A figure of a lion was placed in front of the building.
10. Frogs live in fresh water.

Can you answer these questions?

1. Can you count to five hundred by fives?
2. Can fish really fly?
3. Are you afraid of fire?
4. Can you fry eggs?
5. Can you locate Florida, Frankfort, Fort Ticonderoga and Freeport?

On page 38 you will find some more sentences containing this sound.

31

v is the first sound in "violin." Bite your lower lip with your upper teeth and make a voiced sound.

Say these words aloud, listening for the sound of v.

Group I	*Group II*
violet	several
voice	cover
visit	oven
verb	clover
valentine	river
glove	velvet
leave	sieve
live	sleeve
dive	slave
wave	brave

Repeat each of these phrases three times.

violet velvet	live long	several visitors
very vain	lovely voices	dive bravely
clover leaves	heavy waves	Volga River

32

In these sentences find the words which contain the sound of v. *Then read the sentences aloud.*

1. "Live" and "leave" are verbs.
2. The music of the violin is like a lovely voice.
3. Cover the vegetables before you put them into the oven.
4. Save your steps. Don't leave your playthings on the floor.
5. An active volcano covers its sides with lava.
6. Leave the gloves for David and give the violets to Vera.
7. The ivy is an evergreen vine.
8. The schools receive the parents as visitors during open school week.
9. Clover covered the valley.
10. The Vikings roved all over the seas.

Can you answer these questions?

1. What was the name of the vessel in which Columbus discovered America?
2. Have you ever wished you might voyage with Admiral Byrd?
3. What place would you like to visit during your vacation?
4. What have you read about Paul Revere?
5. What very brave man spent a winter at Valley Forge?

Can you find the sentences on page 38 which contain this sound?

θ is the first sound in "theater." Press the tip of your tongue against the lower edge of your upper front teeth and blow out.

Say these words aloud, listening for the sound of θ.

Group I	Group II
think	method
thumb	arithmetic
thimble	birthday
thirsty	panther
thunder	athletics
north	breath
south	twelfth
youth	sixth
mouth	fifth
cloth	health

Repeat each of these phrases three times.

thirty thimbles	north and south	a twelfth breath
health is wealth	three times	a thirsty panther
think of something	thirty-three	thick cloth
	through thick and thin	

34

In these sentences find the words which contain the sound of
θ. *Then read the sentences aloud.*

1. Thistles pricked his thumb.
2. Clean teeth make a pretty mouth.
3. Thelma had a party on her sixth birthday.
4. Throw the moth through the doorway.
5. Thread and a thimble are needed for sewing cloth.
6. Thursday is the fifth of the month.
7. Thank your sister for her theater party.
8. Thunder and lightning are caused by disturbances in the ether.
9. Thirty thousand Boy Scouts marched through the city streets.
10. A panther has sharp teeth.

Can you answer these questions?

1. Can you say the "three times table"?
2. What country is bounded on the north by Canada and on the south by Mexico?
3. How long can you hold your breath?
4. If a book is three inches wide and the length is twice the width, how long is it?
5. Is strength needed for throwing the discus?

If you need more practice on this sound, turn to page 38.

ð is the third sound in "feathers." Press the tip of your tongue against your upper teeth as you did for θ, but this time make a voiced sound.

Say these words aloud, listening for the sound of ð.

Group I	Group II
these	bathe
them	breathe
that	wreathe
than	clothes
there	with
other	themselves
either	weather
thither	whether
brother	lather
rather	leather

Repeat each of these phrases three times.

mother and father	either one or the other
this rather than that	don't bother your mother
hither and thither	without them
the other wreaths	my other brother
southern clothes	

36

In these sentences find the words which contain the sound of đ.   Then read the sentences aloud.

1. These are the new southern clothes.
2. Breathe deeply though the weather be cold.
3. Is that your brother with your father?
4. The leather in these gloves is thicker than in those.
5. The lake was so smooth that the children wanted to bathe in it.
6. Either of those will do.
7. The horse and the rider were covered with lather.
8. Birds of a feather flock together.
9. It is cold within the caves whether or not the weather is warm without.
10. Although the rose was withered, it still smelled rather sweet.

Can you answer these questions?

1. Would you rather have the weather warm or cold?
2. Do you know what heather is?
3. Can you name two articles of clothing which are made of leather?
4. Have you any brothers?
5. What is the southern boundary of your state?

If you need more practice on this sound, turn to page 38.

Review of the Lip, Teeth, Tongue Sounds

f, v, θ, đ

1. This is the fourth violet I have found.
2. Fetch me a vase for these flowers.
3. These three vegetables have starch in them.
4. What other vines besides wistaria have lavender flowers?
5. The French people think that their country is most beautiful.
6. There are at least three months of snow each year.
7. The fourteenth of February is St. Valentine's Day.
8. The five friends visited the fort.
9. Do you think that there are people living on the moon?
10. Flora picked some fresh tomatoes from the vines.
11. Vera gathered fresh fruit and flowers from the garden.
12. Mother and father visited some friends in Florida.
13. Duluth is a very fine city.
14. Dorothy thought the arithmetic lesson was easy.
15. That is the third fire which we have had this year.
16. Think fast and move quickly during a fire drill.
17. Thank your hostess for the pleasant party.
18. Leave the food on the table and put the other bundles on the floor.
19. Frank played the flute while Bertha played the violin.
20. This is the shortest way from the veranda to the foot of the hill.

21. We wish to win a victory.
22. The wind was very warm.
23. We walked very slowly westward toward Virginia.
24. We went to Vermont with Veronica and William.
25. Wherever we found warm weather, we found worth-less vegetables and wilted flowers.
26. The vines on the south side of the house have thick leaves.
27. There is a fine view of Bear Mountain from the river.
28. In the warm weather it is very refreshing to bathe in the lake.
29. Travelers in Havana find much fun in watching the native boys dive for coins.
30. If you are thirsty, here is a spring of fresh water.
31. There is a time for thought and a time for action.
32. Four chairs were placed under the trees.
33. The flowers of the white heather are supposed to bring good fortune to the wearer.
34. Have you any fresh fish in this store?
35. Yes. We have flounders, fluke, and very nice mackerel.
36. Let me have some of the flounders and three soft-shell crabs.
37. The three boys swam to the raft even though the waves were breaking over it.
38. Have you ever played the vegetable game? It is lots of fun when everyone plays.
39. Have you ever played in a cave at the seashore?
40. Pirates used to hide their gold and other treasures in caves.

t is the first sound in "tennis." Touch the tip of your tongue to the roof of your mouth just behind the upper front teeth. Now blow the tongue down quickly with the breath. *Caution:* Do not touch the tongue tip to the teeth.

Say these words aloud, listening for the sound of t.

Group I	Group II
tent	beast
tiger	felt
time	height
tower	knight
table	totem
west	rattle
kept	potato
heat	butter
heart	later
suit	untie

Repeat each of these phrases three times.

tea for two	east and west	terrible trouble
time to retire	time and tide	twenty-two trees
tall towers	tried and true	heart beats

40

In these sentences find the words which contain the sound of t. Then read the sentences aloud.

1. The Indians built their tents of skins.
2. The highest tower in America is on the Empire State Building.
3. The tiger is a terrible animal.
4. Traders tried to tempt the savages with trinkets.
5. In the Far East, temples were raised to the gods.
6. Two taxicabs were trying to drive down a quiet street.
7. The knights fought for the right.
8. Travelers often tell thrilling tales of adventure.
9. The waiter put the butter on the platter.
10. The little kitten was sitting on the step.

Can you answer these questions?

1. Can you add twelve and twenty-two?
2. Do you like sweet chocolate?
3. Can you tell time?
4. What is a totem pole?
5. Do potatoes and bread contain starch?

Can you find which sentences on page 50 contain this sound?

Note: There are two ways of saying the sound of t. You can find out more about this on page 148.

d is the first sound in "David." Touch the tongue tip to the roof of your mouth as you did for t, but now blow it down with a voiced breath. *Caution:* Do not let the tongue tip touch the teeth.

Say these words aloud, listening for the sound of d.

Group I	Group II
deep	bread
dig	cloud
dog	hundred
dare	meadow
doll	ladder
cold	reduce
bead	indeed
hid	ready
loud	radio
fed	divide

Repeat each of these phrases three times.

dare to do	dance of the dandelions	dots and dashes
dark and dreary	Drake's drum	cold drink
ding dong dell	dig down deep	a hundred days

In these sentences find the words which contain the sound of d.   *Then read the sentences aloud.*

1. The dog hid in the dark corner.
2. The meadow was filled with daisies.
3. The children tried to carry the firewood home.
4. Dora was threading beads to wear on her red dress.
5. Bread and butter help to make red blood.
6. The daffodils danced in the sun.
7. Would you like to ride down into the Grand Canyon?
8. Dorothy heard the program broadcast on the radio.
9. The thunder cloud darkened the sky.
10. Shut the outside door and draw the curtains.

Can you answer these questions?

1. What is David doing in the picture?
2. Why did David do this?
3. Do you like dogs?
4. Whom do you like to hear on the radio?
5. Can you find South Dakota and Denver on the map?

Careless speakers sometimes say d *for* t *when it occurs in the middle of a word.   Can you get* 100% *in the following test?*

better	*not*	bedder
writer	*not*	wrider
city	*not*	cidy
metal	*not*	medal

On page 50 you will find some more sentences containing this sound.

n is the first sound in "news."   Put the tip of the tongue
on the roof of your mouth just as you did for t and d.   Hold
it there while you make a voiced sound through your nose.
Do not let the tongue tip touch the teeth.

Say these words aloud, listening for the sound of n.

Group I	Group II
name	finish
night	fancy
nail	answer
neat	under
next	mountain
number	sound
fun	journey
gain	nine
mine	sunshine
lean	change

Repeat each of these phrases three times.

nice and new	under the sun	journey's end
next number	the fun has begun	lend a hand
ninety-nine	night and noon	noisy neighbors

44

In these sentences find the words which contain the sound of n. *Then read the sentences aloud.*

1. No news was sent for nineteen days.
2. Pansies and petunias grew in the garden.
3. The hunter found a nest of snakes among the rocks.
4. There is nothing new under the sun.
5. The children climbed the mountain.
6. Nuts and raisins are nice for dinner.
7. Both men and women are apt to sunburn in summer.
8. Vancouver is a city in Canada.
9. Nebraska, Nevada, and Wisconsin are in the United States.
10. Neither rain nor sun can stop the trains from running.

Can you answer these questions?

1. When does the school term end?
2. How did young Indian boys learn to become good hunters?
3. Where are the Green Mountains?
4. Have you ever climbed a mountain?
5. Is London bigger than New York?

Can you find the sentences on page 50 which contain this sound?

as in lion

l is the first sound in "lion." Raise the front of your tongue to the roof of your mouth so that the under part touches your upper front teeth. Spread it until the sides of the tongue touch the side teeth. Now make a voiced sound over the sides of the raised tongue.

Say these words aloud, listening for the sound of l.

Group I	Group II
leaf	smell
lost	tell
log	call
light	well
lake	mail
lily	flew
yellow	play
elbow	class
color	shelf
wolf	lull

Repeat each of these phrases three times.

little lilies	linger longer	Lullaby Lou
yellow leaves	lift the latch	toll the bell
long lost	left alone	tell the tale

46

In these sentences find the words which contain the sound of l. Then read the sentences aloud.

1. In the fall the leaves turn yellow.
2. William told Sally about his travels in Ireland.
3. Louise likes to play with building blocks.
4. Daffodils and tulips are spring flowers.
5. Laura lost her woolen cap while she was sliding on the lake.
6. The foolish little pigs laughed at the hungry wolf.
7. The children were sleigh-riding on the hill.
8. The loose snow fell off the roof with a loud sound.
9. Alice was so late for lunch that her soup was cold.
10. Jelly roll and lemon ice are the desserts that I like best.

Can you answer these questions?

1. Would you like to learn to fly?
2. Can you tell the story of Goldilocks?
3. Can you name the colors of the rainbow?
4. Which of the Great Lakes is the largest?
5. Who fought the Battle of Lexington?

If you need more practice on this sound, turn to page 50.

ɹ is the first and fifth sound in "railroad." Raise the tongue tip toward the roof of your mouth as you did for l. Then instead of touching the teeth and the roof of your mouth, just curl the tongue tip back toward your throat. Make a voiced sound.

Say these words aloud, listening for the sound of ɹ.

Group I	Group II
ride	ferry
rock	fairy
rule	borrow
rough	around
read	parade
frame	grandfather
train	crop
proud	barrier
crown	brown
drive	carrot

Repeat each of these phrases three times.

robin redbreast	angry rooster	pretty prompt
read from the right	very rosy	cherry ripe
red raspberries	green grapes	proud parents

48

In these sentences find the words which contain the sound of ɹ. *Then read the sentences aloud.*

1. Ruth rode Robin around the road.
2. Every race was run promptly.
3. Which would you rather do, read a book or row a boat?
4. Russia is a very cold country.
5. The play began with the ringing of a bell and the raising of the curtain.
6. Robert is growing rhubarb, radishes, and roses in his garden.
7. Riverside Drive runs along the bank of the Hudson River.
8. Grace and Rebecca roller skate around the park every afternoon.
9. The ragged children threw rocks into the river.
10. I like to read about life on a ranch.

Can you answer these questions?

1. Do you belong to the Junior Red Cross?
2. Can a train go as rapidly as an automobile?
3. Why did the fox in the story say the grapes were sour?
4. What American rivers can you name?
5. How far have you traveled on a railroad?

If you need more practice on this sound, turn to page 50.

Review of the Tip of the Tongue Sounds

t, d, n, l, ɹ

1. Today is the twenty-second of October.
2. "The Last Rose of Summer" is the name of an old song.
3. My dog, Rags, is black and white and has curly hair.
4. Ducks like to stay out in the rain.
5. David pulled his sister, Mildred, home on her sled.
6. Nuts and candy were hanging on the Christmas tree.
7. Little Lily is lying in the hammock.
8. Have you ever climbed up into a tree?
9. How do you know when a cat is pleased?
10. Dorothy has a green and blue parrot with red wings.
11. The parrot's name is Larry.
12. He came from the West Indies. Do you know where that is?
13. Date palms grow very tall.
14. The fire engine made a great noise as it rushed down the street.
15. The last girl in each row may collect the drawing papers.
16. An apple a day keeps the doctor away.
17. Tom and Dick went for a walk along the docks.
18. Do you like to ride in the trolley car?
19. Only the best butter is used in this cake.
20. Do you know how to catch frogs with a piece of red flannel?
21. The fields in Bermuda are white with Easter lilies.

22. In Italy donkeys are used to pull carts of wood and coal.
23. Let us try to count the stars in the Milky Way.
24. There are so many stars that we shall never finish counting them.
25. Can you find the Great Dipper?
26. When the cherry trees are in bloom, the violets are also flowering.
27. The tulips grow taller than the lilies-of-the-valley.
28. The boy climbed a tree to see the robin's nest.
29. The nest was made of straw and twigs.
30. There were two blue eggs in it.
31. Do you know the story of Swiss Family Robinson?
32. They lived up in a tree as the birds do.
33. The Lady of the Lake was a Scotch girl who loved her country.
34. Today is Mother's Day. We are all writing letters to our mothers.

Here are some words and phrases which you will use in your other school subjects. How many of these can you say correctly?

quotient	battle	multiplicand
Sierra Madre	Saratoga	subtract
volcanic eruption	Lake Louise	noun
	interest	

s is the first sound in "stars." Raise the tongue tip toward the roof of your mouth as though you were going to say t. Then send a small stream of air straight out between your front teeth so that it strikes their cutting edges. *Caution:* Do not let your tongue tip touch your teeth.

Say these words aloud, listening for the sound of s.

Group I	Group II
seat	sister
south	risk
sail	ask
salt	master
nets	custard
loose	snake
geese	skate
place	sea serpent
peace	see saw

Repeat each of these phrases three times.

sing a song of sixpence   lance at rest
sewing a seam   sweeping and dusting
safe and sound   thus and so
the summer sun   a twist of the wrist

In these sentences find the words which contain the sound of s. *Then read the sentences aloud.*

1. The students skated to school.
2. Sailors tasted the sea water and found it salt.
3. The boys held a scooter race across the street from the school.
4. The strong man lifts the posts easily.
5. Sweet custard and strawberries make a nice dessert.
6. Yesterday was St. Valentine's day.
7. Squirrels like to search for nuts.
8. The skipper shouted, "Full speed ahead!"
9. The stars seem very bright on a clear summer night.
10. Sam and his sister sold some stamps to Russell.

Can you answer these questions?

1. Do you know the story of the prince who was changed into a beast?
2. Have you any sisters?
3. Do you know how to make a snow man?
4. Have you ever seen a circus?
5. Can you name six cities in the United States?

On page 64 you will find some more sentences containing this sound.

53

z is the first sound in "zebra." Place the teeth in the same position as for s. Raise the tongue tip and send a voiced sound through the front teeth.

Say these words aloud, listening for the sound of z.

Group I	Group II
zoo	doze
zinc	nose
zero	does
zinnia	joins
zebra	because
dozen	zephyr
frozen	Xavier
reason	zenith
raisin	zeal
cousin	used

Repeat each of these phrases three times.

red as a rose is
Moses' nose is
handsome is as handsome does
zebras in the zoo

a dozen reasons
the breeze blows
close the doors
buzzing bees

frozen toes

54

In these sentences find the words which contain the sound of z. Then read the sentences aloud.

1. Hazel joins in the songs.
2. Please use the other doors.
3. Zinnias and daisies are easy to grow.
4. The children play indoors with their toys when it rains.
5. The zoo is a pleasant place to visit.
6. Mary's cousin has brought a dozen roses to Aunt Susan.
7. The dog's paws are frozen.
8. Does the breeze cause you to lose your place in the book?
9. Boys should not tease their sisters.
10. Mother praised Caroline's pansies because of their size.

Can you answer these questions?

1. What causes water to freeze?
2. How many toes has a cat?
3. What is maize?
4. What size gloves and shoes do you wear?
5. What is a zephyr?

On page 64 you will find some more sentences containing this sound.

ʃ is the first sound in "ships." Say s again. Then
flatten the sides of the tongue so that the groove down the
center is not so narrow. Now send the breath straight out
between the front teeth. ʃ is not so sharp a sound as s.

Say these words aloud, listening for the sound of ʃ.

Group I	Group II
shoe	fashion
shop	attention
sheep	ocean
share	election
shad	pressure
cash	mention
finish	crush
brush	Prussian
lash	delicious
wish	refreshing

Repeat each of these phrases three times.

shut up the shop	sharp shod
share the sugar	sheltered while shopping
finish the lunch	shepherds watch their sheep
washing the dishes	fresh fish

delicious refreshments

In these sentences find the words which contain the sound of ʃ. *Then read the sentences aloud.*

1. This hash is delicious.
2. Wash the fish if you wish to cook them.
3. Ellen showed us her French shawl.
4. The dog's leash was made of crushed leather.
5. The machine made a shrill buzzing noise.
6. Ashley shrugged his shoulders lazily.
7. The dish dropped with a loud crash.
8. The fisherman caught his fish in the meshes of his net.
9. Ships, shoes, shrimp and shellfish, all begin with the same sound.
10. The rose bushes were crushed by a falling tree.

Can you answer these questions?

1. If you could have three wishes, what would you choose?
2. Can you play push-ball?
3. Why do men shear sheep?
4. Is shad a kind of fish?
5. Do you shine your own shoes?

If you need more practice on this sound, turn to page 64.

ʒ is the fourth sound in "treasure." Place the tongue just as you did for ʃ, but send out a voiced sound.

This sound never occurs at the beginning of an English word.

Say these words aloud, listening for the sound of ʒ.

Group I	Group II
azure	explosion
pleasure	confusion
leisure	garage
decision	prestige
measure	composure
vision	seizure
usual	invasion
division	conclusion

Repeat each of these phrases three times.

usual decisions	invasion of leisure
pleasure in leisure	division of treasure
confusion of vision	Persian pleasure

58

In each of these sentences find the words which contain the sound of ʒ. Then read the sentences aloud.

1. The children had much pleasure on the excursion.
2. Italy is known for her azure skies.
3. The garage mechanic measured the oil.
4. The pirates reached a decision to hunt for the treasure.
5. The division of soldiers marched with unusual precision.
6. Who can measure the length of this garage?
7. "Prestige" is an unusual word.
8. The collision of the two cars caused an explosion.
9. The sudden invasion of the Prussian army caused great confusion in Belgium.
10. During the confusion which followed the explosion, no one noticed the seizure of the treasure.

Can you answer these questions?

1. What game gives you the most pleasure?
2. Where is the Treasury Building?
3. What is a mirage?
4. How would you measure your classroom?
5. What was ambrosia?

On page 64 you will find some more sentences containing this sound.

tʃ is the first sound in "chariot." Raise the tip of the tongue as though you were going to say t. Then go rapidly into the sound of ʃ, as in "ships."

Say these words aloud, listening for the sound of tʃ.

Group I	Group II
chimes	merchant
chase	searching
chicken	handkerchief
cheese	exchange
chair	purchase
rich	question
stretch	lecture
church	fixture
reach	chapter
match	checkers

Repeat each of these phrases three times.

chase the chickens   catch the chalk
watch the pitcher   cheer for the chief
search for the handkerchief   peach orchard
in charge of children   kitchen chairs
            chop the cherry tree

60

In these sentences find the words which contain the sound of tʃ. *Then read the sentences aloud.*

1. Place the matches out of reach on the kitchen shelf.
2. Children often teach each other to swim.
3. The chimes in the church tower rang out each hour.
4. Which of the chess players is the champion?
5. The boy chose a handkerchief to match his socks.
6. Charles and his chum like to play checkers.
7. The butcher cut the chops for the child.
8. Touch each word which rhymes with "such."
9. The little chickens hatched out of the eggs.
10. The rich robe reached to the girl's chin.

Can you answer these questions?

1. Which do you like better—peaches or cherries?
2. In what story does the Cheshire cat appear?
3. What is a chariot?
4. Where is Chile?
5. Who was Richard the Lion-Hearted?

If you need more practice on this sound, turn to page 64.

dʒ is the first sound in "jump." Raise the tongue as though you were going to say d. Then go rapidly into the sound of ʒ, as in "treasure."

Say these words aloud, listening for the sound of dʒ.

Group I	*Group II*
judge	strange
gentle	urgent
jacket	pageant
jam	fragile
jaw	orange
college	rejoice
cottage	conjure
dodge	arrange
hedge	geranium
nudge	huge

Repeat each of these phrases three times.

jelly and jam   Japanese jugglers
gorgeous jewels   Johnny-jump-up
dodge through the hedge   badge of courage
gentle Julia   just a joke
             the edge of the bridge

In these sentences find the words which contain the sound of dʒ. *Then read the sentences aloud.*

1. The cottage stood on the edge of a large wood.
2. George and James jumped over the hedge.
3. Jack climbed up to the giant's castle.
4. General Jackson ordered the cavalry to charge.
5. The giraffe is a huge animal.
6. Gypsies journey about in large caravans.
7. Mother gave me some jars of orange jelly.
8. Jimmy enjoyed Joseph's joke.
9. Jack and Jill played a jolly game of magic buttons.
10. Jerry studied his geography.

Can you answer these questions?

1. Do you study geography?
2. Have you ever seen a jellyfish?
3. Where does jasmine grow?
4. Which is larger—Germany or Switzerland?
5. What kind of an animal is a jaguar?

Can you tell which sentences on page 64 contain this sound?

Review of the Sibilant Sounds

s, z, ʃ, ʒ, tʃ, dʒ

1. The sailor saw the North Star in the sky.
2. She wished to share her sugar buns.
3. Each watch was attached to a silk ribbon.
4. Let us have fresh peas and spinach for lunch.
5. George joined the Marines in June.
6. Children seem to enjoy marching and singing.
7. Place these delicious cherries in the silver dish on the side table.
8. Practice makes good speech better.
9. Stella stared at the sparkling stones in the jeweler's window.
10. Spanish houses seem most lovely in the southern states.
11. Muzzle your dogs or the police may arrest you.
12. The question of the excursion was discussed at the first meeting of the society.
13. The cars crashed at the crossing of the two busy streets.
14. Business men often seem stern.
15. The daisies and buttercups were scattered through the grass.
16. The sun was shining as the girls started out on their hike.
17. Have you ever gathered sea shells on the shore?
18. Place your books safely in your desks before you start to use your paints.
19. These oranges are sweeter than those we had yesterday.

20. A gentleman always takes off his hat when he meets a lady.
21. It is as much fun to swim in the summer time as it is to skate in winter.
22. This lace comes from the South of France.
23. Do you like these white grapes as much as the black ones?
24. Bees buzz among the clover blossoms.
25. How much money do you need to buy six dozen eggs?
26. Do you find pleasure in looking at pictures?
27. The ice was so thin that it seemed to be cracking as the skaters passed over it.
28. Such ice is dangerous.
29. The leaves on the trees were stirred by the breeze.
30. Which color do you like best?
31. Vienna is a beautiful city in Austria. The river Danube flows through the city.
32. The frost draws pretty pictures on the window panes.
33. Asters and zinnias blazed in the garden.
34. The children were skipping rope and playing jacks on the sidewalk.
35. Just as Douglas reached the place where Edith stood, the rain began.

Can you find two words in each of your other school subjects which have any of these sibilant sounds in them? Make a list and practice them aloud.

j is the first sound in "yesterday." Raise the middle of your tongue toward the roof of your mouth and blow it down with a voiced breath.

Say these words, listening for the sound of j.

Group I	Group II
yesterday	Tuesday
young	unite
yacht	tune
yard	nuisance
yawn	loyal
yarn	suit
yawl	beyond
yellow	educate
genuine	union
year	million

Repeat each of these phrases three times.

yellow yarn	yield to youth	young yachtsman
yesterday's news	new year	new tunes
the royal yacht	New York	a million onions every year

66

In these sentences find the words which contain the sound of j.
Then read the sentences aloud.

1. Yesterday was Tuesday, January third.
2. The yacht sailed out beyond the lighthouse.
3. Yetta wore a yellow dress with a lace yoke.
4. Julia was sent for a yard of yellow silk and a ball of brown yarn.
5. Daniel's sister is younger than he is.
6. A yawl is a sailboat which has two masts.
7. The crowd yelled when the champion appeared.
8. There are more than a million Italians in the United States.
9. The Yucca plants grow near the Grand Canyon.
10. Your education depends on you.

Can you answer these questions?

1. What color is the yolk of an egg?
2. How many thousands are there in a million?
3. Why do onions make you cry?
4. Do you know what a yeoman was?
5. To what country does Hawaii belong?

On page 80 you will find some more sentences containing this sound.

k is the first sound in "kite." Raise the back of your tongue to your soft palate. Then blow it down with the breath.

Say these words aloud, listening for the sound of k.

Group I	Group II
key	accident
kind	action
king	company
kindle	lilac
kiss	banquet
castle	crowd
cow	clown
careful	queen
copper	export
cost	exit

Repeat each of these phrases three times.

kill with kindness	cut the corners	cook a cake
careful courtesy	catch the bouquet	copper kettles
clean carpets	count the cost	crown the king

68

In these sentences find the words which contain the sound of k. *Then read the sentences aloud.*

1. Come to the country.
2. Who killed Cock Robin?
3. Cousin Kate comes from Kentucky.
4. A good catcher can catch even a fast ball.
5. The coach showed the boys how to kick the ball.
6. Jack wrote in his book with ink.
7. The children hung their caps and coats on the hooks.
8. Crowds of people were coming to see the clowns tumbling on the carpet.
9. Cut the cake and pass the chicken to Aunt Christina.
10. Kathryn found the kitten curled up under the lilac bush.

Can you answer these questions?

1. What kind of cake do you like best?
2. What is a young cat called?
3. What is a cricket?
4. Who helped Columbus discover America?
5. What is a castle?

On page 80 you will find some more sentences containing this sound.

Note: There are two ways of saying the sound of k. You can find out more about this on page 148.

g is the first sound in "gull." Raise the back of your tongue as for k. Blow it down with a voiced breath.

Say these words aloud, listening for the sound of g.

Group I	Group II
girl	again
games	agate
glad	digger
ghost	youngest
goose	begin
leg	fatigue
stag	catalog
twig	drug
fog	rogues
jug	egg

Repeat each of these phrases three times.

rag bag	again and again	big game
goose eggs	begin again	green grocer
gold digger	good gray gander	giggling girls

70

In these sentences find the words which contain the sound of g. Then read the sentences aloud.

1. The girls dragged the log toward the gate.
2. Grace is younger than Gladys.
3. The elephant's child came to the "great, gray-green, greasy Limpopo River."
4. Put the green glass goblets on the table.
5. The little goslings were eating the fresh green grass.
6. Give the other girls some of that good, grape jelly.
7. The flowers in the glass jug came from the greenhouse.
8. The dog has been playing on the new grass rug.
9. The captain of the basketball team threw a goal and won the game.
10. Gardenias do not grow in northern gardens.

Can you answer these questions?

1. What games do you like to play?
2. Where is gold found?
3. Do you know what a gopher is?
4. Where does grapefruit grow?
5. What color is a gardenia?

On page 80 you will find some more sentences containing this sound.

ŋ is the third and last sound in "singing." Raise the back of the tongue as for k and g. Hold it against the soft palate while you make a voiced sound through your nose. *Caution:* Be careful not to let the tongue fall until you have stopped making the voiced sound.

Say these words aloud, listening for the sound of ŋ.

Group I	Group II
sing	dancing
wrong	leaping
hang	turning
long	blushing
wing	fencing
ringer	running
singing	walking
swinging	eating
hanging	drinking

Repeat each of these phrases three times.

singing a song	reading a book
walking along	rushing out in the cold
eating an apple	young Americans
running a race	writing on the board

*In these sentences find the words which contain the sound
of ŋ. Then read the sentences aloud.*

1. Sing a song of sixpence.
2. Susan was sitting on a bench in the park.
3. She was feeding acorns to the squirrels.
4. They were eating out of her hand.
5. It was a spring afternoon and the sun was shining.
6. Susan's brother was hitting a ball with a bat.
7. Spot, their dog, was chasing a cat and barking at it.
8. Coming along the path were two little boys eating oranges.
9. Suddenly a little girl came running along crying aloud, "A bee stung me!"
10. A big dog was dragging a small cart after him.

Can you answer these questions?

1. Do you prefer playing baseball to flying a kite?
2. Are you fond of blowing bubbles?
3. To what state does Springfield belong?
4. Have you ever seen a bird's nest hanging from the branch of a tree?
5. Have you ever tried swinging on the flying rings?

Rules for the Pronunciation of ng

These two letters may be pronounced in four ways. Two ways do not give any trouble.

I. In words where the "n" is part of the prefix "con," and the "g" is part of the root word, "ng" is pronounced n+g.

Example: congratulate

II. Where the words end in "nge," the "ng" is pronounced n+dʒ.

Example: fringe, singe, mange

III. Where words end in "ng," or in "ngue," or in "ngth," or in "ngthen," the "ng" is pronounced ŋ. This is just a single, nasal, continuant sound made (see page 72) by pressing the back of the tongue against the soft palate and sending the voice through the nose. There is no "n" and no "g" in these words.

Example: sing, tongue, length, strengthen

Moreover, when the suffix "er," meaning the doer, is added to a word ending in "ng," this word also is pronounced ŋ.

Example: sing—singer, ring—ringer

There are three exceptions. Learn them.
lɒŋ—lɒŋgə, lɒŋgɪst—long, longer, longest
stɹɒŋ—stɹɒŋgə, stɹɒŋgɪst—strong, stronger, strongest
jʌŋ—jʌŋgə, jʌŋgɪst—young, younger, youngest.

74

IV. In all other cases "ng" in the middle of a word is pronounced ŋ+g.

Example: finger, single, tangle, linger

Learn these two exceptions: Bingham and gingham follow Rule III and are pronounced bɪŋəm and gɪŋəm.

Here are some phrases containing the single sound ŋ.

ringing a bell	swinging on the gate
dancing at home	among other things
bringing in the paper	asking a question

Here are some phrases containing the double sound ŋ+g.

tangled footsteps	mingle with the crowd
to tingle with anger	to linger after school
hungry people	angry mobs

Here are some phrases containing both sounds. Can you tell which sound to use?

mingling with the dancers	sulking angrily
hungry from fasting	every single young American
lingering at home	singing by the strongest voices

Which words in the following list are pronounced with ŋ alone, which with ŋg, which with ndʒ and which with ŋk? Repeat the rule which applies in each case.

mangle	triangle	spank	hanger	language
younger	angle	prink	hangar	frankly
rushing	manger	longest	English	spangled
bringing	cringing	gingham	languid	inkling
bangle	sinking	clangor	twinges	linger

75

Additional Practice on ŋ, ŋg, ŋk, ndʒ

Say these words aloud, listening for the sounds of ŋ, ŋg, ŋk, ndʒ.

hunger	jingling	thinker
finger	spangle	monkey
angry	twinkle	donkey
single	linger	sponge
tangle	stronger	fringe
dangling	bungler	sings
longest	ink	strange
younger	sinking	plunge

Repeat each of these phrases three times.

the youngest and the strongest   sinking into inky water
they hold out the longest   plunge into the strange water
dingle dongle bell   don't sing
tingle tangle tangle foot   your fringe
twinkle, twinkle, little star

In these sentences find the words which contain the sound of ŋ *or* ŋg *or* ŋk *or* ndʒ. *Then read the sentences aloud.*

1. The hungry monkeys hung by their long tails to the strongest limbs.
2. The boys plunged into the water in search of sponges.
3. The bells jingled as the riders were sprinkled with snow from the horses' hoofs.
4. The donkey is a strange animal.
5. The class sang a verse from the "Star Spangled Banner."

76

6. The kindergarten children were stringing pop corn.
7. There was not a single star in the sky.
8. John is younger than Henry but he is the strongest boy in the family.
9. The lights on the boat twinkled merrily.
10. The stranger proved stronger than his enemy.

Rewrite the list of words on page 76 in four lists according to the sound of ng.

In List 1, place all the words in which ng has the sound of ŋ; in List 2, the words in which ng has the sound of ŋg; in List 3, the words in which ng has the sound of ŋk; in List 4, the words in which ng has the sound of ndʒ.

If any word contains two sounds, put it in both lists. When you have finished, check your answers with the lists on page 81.

Can you answer these questions?

1. Can you write with ink?
2. Do you like to untangle cord?
3. Which is longer, a yard or a rod?
4. Which of your fingers is the longest?
5. What animals live in the jungle?

h is the first sound in "horse."   Just open your mouth and sigh.

Say these words aloud, listening for the sound of h.

Group I	Group II
have	inhale
hear	behave
hatter	behead
home	behold
hut	beehive
hatch	rehearse
happy	adhere
harp	hasty
hunt	hatchet
help	haul

Repeat each of these phrases three times.

heart and home   have and hold   handsome horses
heavy handed   humble home   hot houses
hot headed   hail the hero   Hark, hark, the lark

In these sentences find the words which contain the sound of h.
Then read the sentences aloud.

1. Hold your head high and fear no one.
2. Harry overturned the beehive. Then he hurried away.
3. The horses were hot because their load was heavy.
4. Hold your chest high and inhale slowly.
5. The boys hurried home because they were hungry.
6. Horses are used for hunting and for hauling heavy loads.
7. Do not try to hold yourself on a ladder without using both hands.
8. This hammock is hung in the shade of the house.
9. The hawk swooped down and took hold of a hen.
10. Hazel had a hole in the heel of her stocking.

Can you answer these questions?

1. What river did Henry Hudson discover?
2. Who chopped down a cherry tree with his new hatchet?
3. Whose horse was called Blueskin?
4. How many hundreds are there in a thousand?
5. Have you ever seen a humming bird?

If you need more practice on this sound, turn to page 80.

Some sounds of speech make use of the vocal cords; they are called voiced sounds. Some sounds are made up with no vibration from the strings; they are called voiceless sounds. Turn to the inside front cover of this book and go through the list of sounds given there. See whether you can tell which of them are voiced and which are voiceless. It will help you to do this to put your fingers in your ears and speak the sounds aloud. The voiced sounds will be very loud, and the unvoiced sounds will be scarcely heard. Then try reading a paragraph whispering the words, your fingers still in your ears. Notice that certain pairs of sounds that were very different, when spoken aloud, are now quite similar to each other. Can you work out these pairs?

Review

j, k, g, h

1. Kate caught cold.
2. The kittens climbed up into the grape arbor.
3. The candles were lighted high up on the tree.
4. It is cold in the gold fields.
5. Golf is a good game.
6. How high is the house in which you live?
7. Come out of the cold air into the house.
8. The clock was beginning to strike the hour.
9. Cinderella ran down the steps of the castle looking for her pumpkin carriage.
10. She dropped her glass slipper on the ground.
11. Her beautiful clothes began to change back into rags.
12. Do you know where gold comes from?
13. Have you ever heard of the Klondike?
14. High up in the Rocky Mountains there is a glacier. Do you know what that is?
15. A great honeysuckle vine hung over the gate.
16. What do you do with a hatchet? With a hoe? With a hammer?
17. "The horn of the hunter is heard on the hill."
18. Helen hurried home to help her mother.
19. Figs and dates grow in warm countries.
20. Grace drank her milk gladly.

80

21. The girls picked the black grapes and placed them in baskets.
22. The frogs were croaking in the dark.
23. The gardener caught a gray mole.
24. Acorns grow on oak trees.
25. Where are those crowds of gay people going?
26. The youngest girl carried a handful of yellow buttercups.
27. Yesterday was New Year's Day.
28. The great, tall building cast a long shadow on the ground.
29. Are you going to our camp this year?
30. Take care not to get your feet wet or you may catch a cold.

Review of familiar words found in other school subjects:

1. How many k sounds in "Mexico"?
2. What is the second sound in "Guatemala"?
3. What is an isthmus? How many sounds are there in the word "isthmus"?
4. Say a word which contains the same sound as the g in "percentage."

Answers to test on page 77.

ŋ — dangling, jingling, sinking, sings

ŋg — hunger, finger, angry, single, tangle, dangling, longest, younger, stronger, jingling, spangle, linger, bungler

ŋk — ink, sinking, thinker, monkey, donkey

ndʒ — sponge, fringe, strange, plunge

81

The Sounds
of
English

II. Vowels

iː is the first sound in "eagle." Spread your lips in a smile and raise the front of your tongue toward the roof of your mouth.

Make a voiced sound for all vowels.

Say these words aloud, listening for the sound of iː.

Group I	Group II
eel	league
seed	referee
team	beechnut
feel	belief
bead	meter
receive	steal
increase	freeze
people	please
peanut	preach
complete	streak

Repeat each of these phrases three times.

leaves of trees	peaceful seas
weak tea	steel beads
feel the breeze	see the bees

84

In these sentences find the words which contain the sound of iː. *Then read the sentences aloud.*

1. Please do not tease Lena.
2. Edith has the measles.
3. We need three needles and some green thread.
4. We shall sow these seeds under the fruit trees.
5. Each creature seeks to find enough to eat.
6. Edam cheese comes from Holland.
7. Peter teased the girls easily.
8. The queen bee flew east.
9. Each evening the mother seal swam out to sea to seek for food.
10. The sidewalk feels hard under our heels.

Can you answer these questions?

1. What is the eagle in the center of the picture doing?
2. How many eagles are there in the picture?
3. Have you ever seen an eagle?
4. Can you see any sheep in the picture?
5. Would you scream if you saw an eagle?

If you can answer all these questions, turn to page 96 and read aloud all the words which have the sound of iː *in them.*

ɪ is the second sound in "city." It is a high front vowel. Put your tongue in the position for iː but do not let it stiffen.

Say these words aloud, listening for the sound of ɪ.

Group I	*Group II*
sit	Indian
hid	wishes
rip	whipping
did	singing
pitch	tinkle
kitchen	insist
gypsy	artist
thimble	pity
nibble	little
mill	business

Repeat each of these phrases three times.

big city	give gifts	hidden riches
little stitches	silk ribbons	fill the bill
silver thimble	pretty kittens	silly children

In these sentences find the words which contain the sound of ɪ. *Then read the sentences aloud.*

1. William hid the rabbit under the kitchen sink.
2. Did Richard bring enough cake for six people?
3. Which bridge did Paul Revere ride over?
4. Children still like to hear the story of the three little pigs.
5. Dicky listened while his sister sang.
6. This string is six inches long.
7. You must be quick if you want to do tricks.
8. Sylvia knitted six silk sweaters for Christmas.
9. Jimmy built a house of sticks.
10. Did you ever fish with a pin?

If you can read the next sentences, do what they tell you to do.

1. Whistle "Dixie."
2. Tell a riddle.
3. Skip six times without missing once.
4. Fill in the missing word in this proverb. "A......in time saves nine."

If you need more practice on this sound, turn to page 96.

87

as in elephant

ĕᴛ is the first sound in "elephant." Put your tongue in the position for ɪ, then lower it a little bit. Be careful not to lower the tongue too much. Keep the tip of the tongue lightly pressed against the back of the lower front teeth.

Say these words aloud, listening for the sound of ĕᴛ.

Group I	Group II
end	seven
help	shed
edge	tremble
egg	athletic
tell	dress
met	repent
energy	friend
insect	meadow
beggar	twenty
enter	central

Repeat each of these phrases three times.

red head	heavy weather	friendly enemy
dead end	beg for bread	send help
twenty men	electric engines	ten lemons

In these sentences find the words which contain the sound of ет. *Then read the sentences aloud.*

1. Fred went to the end of the garden where there was a bend in the path.
2. Betty lent Greta seven eggs.
3. When Jennie went to Belgium, she was compelled to get a passport.
4. Nettie wore a red dress and a velvet hat with a small feather.
5. Henry spent seventy cents for twelve red pencils.
6. Bessie helped the beggar.
7. Spot, the terrier, rested his head on Teddy's knee.
8. Kim sat right up on the elephant's neck.
9. They watched the red sunset from the deck of the ferry.
10. Edna said she wanted some salt but she took some pepper instead.

Can you answer these questions?

1. What colors do leaves turn in the fall?
2. Where do elephants live?
3. What are the men doing in the picture?
4. What athletic sport do you like best?
5. Can you stand on your left leg?

Can you find which sentences on page 96 have the sound of ет *in them?*

ɛɪ is the first sound in "airplane." Place the tongue in the position for eɪ and then lower it slightly.

Say these words aloud, listening for the sound of ɛɪ.

Group I	Group II
pare	repairing
lair	seafaring
hair	snare
tear	preparing
caring	bearing
paring	compare
bare	repair
dare	declare
daring	unfair
heiress	parent

Repeat each of these phrases three times.

come to the fair	beware, take care	there is the heir
wear and tear	snare the hare	daring airmen
here and there	prepare to share	in the glare of the flares

90

In these sentences find the words which contain the sound of ει.   *Then read the sentences aloud.*

1. Wear this pair of gloves.
2. Compare this pear with that one.
3. Parents and children should share their pleasures.
4. Do you care for fairy stories?
5. Can you compare the word "rare"?
6. Only the brave deserve the fair.
7. Where can you buy a pair of shoes?
8. There's where the West begins.
9. Air and sunshine share in building health.
10. A lair is a cave where a wild animal lives.

Can you answer these questions?

1. Would you care to ride in an airplane?
2. What is the name of a rigid airship?
3. Can you name three famous airmen?
4. Why should we breathe fresh air?
5. What share do you take in the care of your room?

If you need more practice on this sound, turn to page 96.

æ is the first sound in "apple." Open your mouth a little more than you did for ɛɪ. Be sure to let the sound come through your mouth rather than through your nose.

Say these words aloud, listening for the sound of æ.

Group I	Group II
bat	crash
candy	cabbage
had	mantle
lamb	stamp
sack	match
caddy	capacity
handsome	companion
wagon	savage
dagger	passage
happy	frantic

Repeat each of these phrases three times.

bag and baggage	band wagon	black cats
hand in hand	cash and carry	Jack Spratt
black and tan	hat stand	happy man

92

In these sentences find the words which contain the sound of æ. Then read the sentences aloud.

1. Jack had a new bat and ball.
2. The bad man stole a sack of corn.
3. Marion sat with her back to the door.
4. Mary had a lamb that ate candy and a rabbit that ate grass.
5. Watch the acrobat hang from the flying ring.
6. Have you ever seen the big waves crash on the shore?
7. Harriet's mother had a black hat and carried a black bag.
8. Mattie had a hatchet in one hand and a can of oil in the other.
9. At camp we gathered around the fire and sang songs.
10. Adam ate the apple that Eve gave him.

Can you answer these questions?

1. Can you play "catch as catch can"?
2. Can you add twelve and five?
3. Would you like to drive a taxicab?
4. Can you paddle a canoe?
5. Can you make shadow pictures?

If you need more practice on this sound, turn to page 96.

ɑ is the second sound in "dance." This is the lowest of the front vowels. Open your mouth a little more than you did for æ. Be sure to keep the back of your tongue slightly raised so that the sound is farther forward than the ɑɪ in "garden."

Say these words, listening for sound of ɑ.

Group I	*Group II*
ask	planting
fast	dancing
class	grant
path	command
laugh	demand
grasp	branch
grass	chance
glance	example
France	draft
lance	clasp

Repeat each of these phrases three times.

the last laugh	half past eight	the lances of France
the grassy path	pass your glass	plant the grass
ask the class	demand an answer	the last example

94

In these sentences find the words which contain the sound of a. *Then read the sentences aloud.*

1. He who laughs last laughs best.
2. At last we found the path.
3. Francis grasped the branch that hung over the path.
4. The Basques dance very fast.
5. Begin to do the example as soon as you hear the command.
6. What is the last sound in "draft"?
7. The dancing master asked the class to repeat the last dance.
8. The girls put some flowering plants and some evergreen branches in the Christmas baskets.
9. The girls passed their glasses for more lemonade.
10. Now is your last chance to ask a question.

Can you answer these questions?

1. How many plants are there in your nature room?
2. How many examples did you finish last night?
3. How many dancers can you count in the picture?
4. Have you ever cut grass?
5. Which task do you dislike most?

Can you find which sentences on page 96 contain this sound?

Review of the Front Vowels

ıː, ɪ, eɪ, ɛː, æ, a

1. We need neither food nor sleep.
2. It is a pity that city children lack play space.
3. Did you get your croquet set wet yesterday, Nettie?
4. Where there's a will, there's a way.
5. Jack put his hat on the rack and sat down.
6. The dance was held on the grass.
7. Jean hid the pebbles in the woodshed.
8. Where did Melissa get a hair net?
9. There is the path where Betty met the black cat.
10. Frieda's pet kitten fell in the pan of milk.
11. This is the last class to pass down the back stairs.
12. When did she get back from France?
13. Let me see where the glasses are.
14. In a pretty little western city there is a big hickory tree.
15. Will you please fix this tire quickly?
16. In summer we wear bathing suits all day and go barefoot.
17. The last man ran forward quickly and met the rest of his friends at the barrier.
18. Marie sat on a bench, tatting a collar for Helen's dress.
19. Henry's ball fell against the tennis net.

20. Don't wear your best clothes when you climb the pear tree.
21. The half-back caught the ball and began running with it.
22. Take care in walking down the icy stairs.
23. The man was sent to jail for passing bad checks.
24. The lily-of-the-valley smells very sweet.
25. Canada is a British dominion.
26. We live in the western hemisphere.
27. Bears like to eat honey and candy.
28. Goldilocks sat in the chairs that belonged to the three bears.
29. Mary has a pretty, green dress with a silk sash.
30. Fresh eggs are cheap now.
31. Here is a list of the things we shall need for the dance.
32. When shall we three meet again?
33. Have you ever seen a brown bear in the park?
34. When the spring comes, the birds begin to build their nests in the cherry trees.
35. Betty and her friends are knitting sweaters.
36. Mary's sweater is yellow, with green collar and cuffs.
37. Helen is knitting a cap to match her sweater. It is pink.
38. The girls plan to wear their new sweaters when they go to the beach to swim.
39. Our class is going to have a party on the last day in September.
40. We are writing invitations to our teacher and the principal.

ɜː is the second sound in "world." Raise the middle of your tongue toward the roof of your mouth. Touch the tip lightly to the back of your lower front teeth. Let your lips hang naturally; do not round them.

Say these words aloud, listening for the sound of ɜː.

Group I	Group II
bird	world
turn	verse
earth	worse
word	earnest
her	furniture
fern	occur
burn	refer
return	concern
learning	converse
early	burning

Repeat each of these phrases three times.

the first worm	girls with curls	turn the fern
the earth turns	the early bird	learn to churn
worse and worse	learn this verse	return the purse

In these sentences find the words which contain the sound of ɜ:. *Then read the sentences aloud.*

1. The girl wore a white shirtwaist and a plaid skirt.
2. Draw a circle in the earth.
3. Thirty squirrels were used in this fur coat.
4. What is the first sound in "earn"?
5. This term we are learning some memory gems from "The Child's Garden of Verse."
6. Bertha searched in the woods for ferns.
7. Some girls learn to speak German well.
8. The first and third words could not be heard.
9. Myrtle stirred the pudding so it would not burn.
10. Do not disturb the birds who are perched on the tree.

Can you answer these questions?

1. What is the meaning of the word "converse"?
2. Who was the first President of the United States?
3. Does wood burn best when it is wet or dry?
4. Are girls as smart as boys?
5. What is the use of a thermos bottle?

For additional practice in this sound, turn to page 114.

ə is the first sound in "abroad." It is used in unstressed syllables and in diphthongs. If you do not know what unstressed syllables are, you can find out on page 152. Place the tongue as for ɜː but let all the energy go out of it.

Say these words aloud, listening for the sound of ə.

Group I	Group II
among	wonderful
alone	national
around	capital
upon	mortal
confess	Indian
extra	cinnamon
zebra	diamond
soda	canary
comfort	autumn
sofa	separate

Repeat each of these phrases three times.

about a million   avoid the piazza   vanilla sodas
comfortable sofa   the national capitol among the Indians
open the umbrella   aroma of onions   Havana, Cuba

100

In these sentences find the words which contain the sound of ə. Then read the sentences aloud.

1. The policeman and the fireman went around the corner together.
2. The waiter served cinnamon buns and chocolate.
3. Two West Point cadets received medals for bravery.
4. There are sixty seconds in each minute.
5. The football player's number was hidden by the referee.
6. Do you prefer strawberry or vanilla ice cream?
7. Martha sent a package by special messenger.
8. Laura visited the opera with her neighbor's daughter.
9. Elephants and lions are found in Africa.
10. Georgia, North and South Carolina, and Florida are all southern states.

Can you answer these questions?

1. Where is Alaska?
3. Who was Ferdinand De Soto?
3. How many square rods are there in an acre?
4. Have you ever seen the wonderful Northern Lights?
5. Where are diamonds found?

If you need more practice on this sound, turn to page 114.

as in umbrella

ʌ is the first sound in "umbrella." It is the lowest middle vowel. It has nearly the same sound as ə but ʌ is used generally in a stressed syllable while ə is used always in unstressed syllables. Be careful not to make this sound too far back in your throat.

Say these words aloud, listening for the sound of ʌ.

Group I	*Group II*
fun	coming
come	lunch
run	touch
mud	rush
rug	stuff
bubble	bundle
huddle	reduction
trouble	function
sudden	result
rough	confront

Repeat each of these phrases three times.

bug in a rug	cut up	crumple up
sudden trouble	come to lunch	a dozen bundles
mud puddle	run to the front	ugly duckling

102

In these sentences find the words which contain the sound of ʌ. Then read the sentences aloud.

1. Duncan fed the monkey with nuts.
2. Mother gave us some money to buy some butter and some honey.
3. Are you coming to the country with us?
4. The mustard stung their tongues.
5. The young hunter fired his gun when he saw the bunny run.
6. Water buffaloes are found in the jungle.
7. Hold your bundle under your arm so that you won't stumble.
8. The summer sun made it too hot for running.
9. The thunder was rumbling so we rushed to get under cover.
10. Don't you wonder how the juggler can avoid stumbling?

Can you answer these questions?

1. How can you develop big muscles?
2. What part of America was settled by the Dutch?
3. Can you tell the story of the Ugly Duckling?
4. What has happened to the boy's umbrella in this picture?
5. Is the little dog hungry or afraid?

Can you tell which sentences on page 114 contain this sound?

u: is the second sound in "tools." It is the highest back vowel. Round your lips until they make a small circle. Now raise the back of your tongue and make a voiced sound.

Say these words aloud, listening for the sound of u:.

Group I	Group II
soon	hoop
school	goose
shoe	plume
rule	shrewd
noon	prudent
soup	balloon
route	typhoon
bruises	monsoon
spool	lagoon
truth	remove

Repeat each of these phrases three times.

school shoes   June moon   a cool pool
soup spoon   loose the noose   tootle the flute
your food   fruit juice   remove the screw

104

In these sentences find the words which contain the sound of uː. *Then read the sentences aloud.*

1. Whose shoes are in that room?
2. When the noon whistle blew, the workmen laid down their tools.
3. Fruit juice is very cooling.
4. Julia wore a blue plume in her hat.
5. Do you like to hunt for goose eggs?
6. The rooster crew early in the morning.
7. It is very rude to blow on your soup to cool it.
8. Two blue herons were given to the zoo.
9. Susan tripped over the root and bruised her knee.
10. The cruel boy tried to shoot the raccoon.

Can you answer these questions?

1. What color would you choose for your room?
2. Do you like to roll a hoop?
3. How many tools can you find in the picture?
4. Are there any stools in this room?
5. Can you name two men who were Presidents of the United States?

Can you find the sentences on page 114 which contain this sound?

ʊ is the second sound in "football." It is made with the tongue and lips in the same position for uː, but the tongue is not so energized. Be sure to keep your lips rounded.

Say these words aloud, listening for the sound of ʊ.

Group I	Group II
book	cushion
foot	mistook
put	crooked
good	woolen
full	bushy
butcher	shook
Brooklyn	could
sugar	pussy
woman	pudding
bushel	wolf

Repeat each of these phrases three times.

good looks	wooden pulley	bushel full
cook book	you could if you would	woolen worsted
push and pull	sugar cookies	good pudding

106

In these sentences find the words which contain the sound of ʊ.
Then read the sentences aloud.

1. The butcher bought the bull calf.
2. The cook shook sugar over the cookies.
3. The girl put a cushion behind her head before she opened her book.
4. We gathered almost a bushel of chestnuts after the boys shook the trees.
5. Could you make a good pudding?
6. Pussy put her foot into the goldfish bowl.
7. The hungry boys came into the kitchen, looking for food.
8. Let us sit here in this shady nook next to the brook.
9. The gardener pulled up the crooked rose bush.
10. A good fisherman likes to fish for brook trout.

Can you answer these questions?

1. Do you like to read a good book?
2. Can you name three berries that grow on bushes?
3. Why do they call them "pussy" willows?
4. Would you rather chop wood or cook?
5. Would you like to be a butcher?

You will find some other sentences containing this sound on page 114.

ɔː is the first sound in "automobile." Round your lips and then pull them down until they make a long opening.

Say these words aloud, listening for the sound of ɔː.

Group I	Group II
tall	report
saw	forty
horn	belongs
haul	almost
score	naughty
quart	autumn
straw	absorb
crawl	cauliflower
squaw	yawn
border	gaudy

Repeat each of these phrases three times.

short or tall	all haul	a waterfall
forty quarts	launch the yawl	a gauze shawl
morning walk	warning call	forward in order

In these sentences find the words which contain the sound of ɔɪ. Then read the sentences aloud.

1. Paul had a new straw hat.
2. The small boy saw a tall man looking at the yawl.
3. This gaudy basket is made of straw.
4. The bird soared almost out of sight.
5. Four small rabbits crawled out of the straw.
6. The horse pawed the ground in front of the store.
7. George bought a watermelon for forty-four cents.
8. The naughty boys were caught and punished.
9. Walter saw a fire and called for help.
10. It is now a quarter before four o'clock.

Can you answer these questions?

1. Can you saw wood for a fire?
2. Do you like to go for a short walk in the morning before school?
3. Would you rather eat watermelon or pop corn?
4. Would you rather walk or ride in an automobile?
5. Would you rather be a flyer or a lawyer?

There are more sentences containing this sound on page 114.

ɒ is the second sound in "golf." Round your lips as you did for ɔː but do not pull them down into such a long mouth. *Note:* Sometimes it helps if you put your mouth in the position for ɔː and then say ɑː as in "garden." Be sure to keep the lips slightly rounded.

Say these words aloud, listening for the sound of ɒ.

Group I	*Group II*
gone	collar
often	block
coffee	frock
wrong	forest
soft	box
belong	stopped
watch	crop
cough	plot
doctor	blossom
cloth	strong

Repeat each of these phrases three times

hot coffee	cloth frock	clock watcher
soft spot	rock cod	orange blossom
strong box	long block	frog pond

110

In these sentences find the words which contain the sound of
ɒ. *Then read the sentences aloud.*

1. Dr. Cox offered to help Dorothy lift the box.
2. The dogwood blossoms in Bronx Park are lovely.
3. The frost made ice form on the pond.
4. Oliver ordered Scotch broth and strong coffee.
5. They washed the table cloth to remove the spot.
6. Tom's dog, Michael, trotted beside him.
7. John sent us a box of codfish from Boston.
8. Polly lost the collar which belonged to her good frock.
9. How many of these problems can you solve?
10. Mary dropped her doll and lost it.

Can you answer these questions?

1. Does your father play golf?
2. What spot near your home is the prettiest?
3. Do you prefer coffee or chocolate ice cream?
4. Do you know what the top of a mountain is called?
5. What is wrong with the answer to this problem? Two and seventeen make twenty.

There are more sentences containing this sound on page 114.

ɑː is the lowest back vowel. Allow your mouth to fall open and your tongue to lie flat in your mouth. *Note:* This is the sound your doctor asks you to make when he wants to look down your throat, because when you say ɑː your throat is wide open and your tongue is flat. ɑː is the second sound in "garden."

Say these words aloud, listening for the sound of ɑː.

Group I	*Group II*
palm	market
farm	dark
father	charge
are	pardon
arch	started
yard	guard
heart	armor
party	argument
barking	largely

Repeat each of these phrases three times.

barnyard	sharp bark	hard hearted
large party	start farming	market cart
guard in armor	dark yarn	park your car

112

In these sentences find the words which contain the sound of ɑ:. *Then read the sentences aloud.*

1. Father started to work in the garden before breakfast.
2. Arthur was invited to a heart party on St. Valentine's Day.
3. A large dog barked as the boys tried to park their car.
4. There are several white swans on the lake in Central Park.
5. The Queen of Hearts made some tarts.
6. Carl had a good report card.
7. The boys built a large cart.
8. The pirates found the treasure chart in a dark corner of the attic.
9. The barber cut Ethel's hair without charge.
10. Archie took his mother's arm to help her along the dark street.

Can you answer these questions?

1. Where is Arkansas?
2. What is an artichoke?
3. Which is the largest state in the Union?
4. Have you ever seen a palm tree?
5. How far is your home from your school?

If you need more practice on this sound, turn to page 114.

Review of the Middle and Back Vowels

ɜɪ, ə, ʌ, uɪ, ʊ, ɔɪ, ɒ, ɑɪ

1. That is the third bluebird which I have seen since Tuesday.
2. Who put all those crumbs on the rug?
3. What would you do with a million dollars?
4. Girls do not wear their hair in long curls any more.
5. Always cut flowers with long stems.
6. Country roads are often rough.
7. Would you like to learn how to churn?
8. You make butter by churning.
9. Paul and his brother hauled the logs from the shore.
10. When you open a new book, turn down a few pages at a time.
11. Nora lost her way in the woods.
12. Her dog, Spot, hunted for her until he found her.
13. When Spot found Nora, he barked and barked.
14. Then Nora's father ran as fast as he could into the woods.
15. Soon he came to the spot where Nora and her dog were sitting.
16. They all walked home happily.
17. Lulu obeyed her mother's call.
18. Susan wanted another doll.
19. Thomas had just come home when Julia called them all to supper.
20. There were large orange dots on Flora's frock.

21. If your cough doesn't improve by morning, we shall call in a doctor.
22. Coffee is not good for young children.
23. Put strong cord around the box.
24. Are you coming to our party on Monday?
25. Always come to the front of the room when you talk.
26. The girls were feeding the bluebirds some crumbs.
27. The crows were calling in the treetops at sunset.
28. Fruit and cake are good for lunch.
29. Come into the nature room to see the new frogs.
30. We are starting a garden in our window boxes.
31. Walter brought a small water snake to school.
32. We put it in the nature room and fed it with meat.
33. Lucy brought some moss for the little pool that we are building in the school garden.
34. We want to have some goldfish and a few turtles in the pool.
35. Where can we find rich earth in which to plant ferns?
36. Along the borders we shall plant daffodils and tulip bulbs.
37. We shall water the grass every day when the weather is warm.
38. We hope that our garden will be awarded first prize.
39. The third-year pupils picked a charming bouquet for the principal's office.
40. Julia wrote a poem about the school garden.

The Sounds of English

III. *Diphthongs*

eɪ is the second sound in "fable." It is a combination of the sound of eʀ in elephant and ɪ as in city. Do not stress the ɪ as you do the eʀ. Practice saying the sound as though it were made with a vowel and a vanish.

Say these words aloud, listening for the sound of eɪ.

Group I	Group II
bay	behave
they	complain
weigh	retrace
navy	milk pail
sail	gain
crave	pavement
brave	laboring
breaking	playful
bracelet	praise
mailman	flavoring

Repeat each of these phrases three times.

way station	save the race	lay the table
praise the players	trace the break	shady place
behave bravely	sail with the navy	cake sale

118

In these sentences find the words which contain the sound of eɪ. *Then read the sentences aloud.*

1. Place the cake on the table.
2. Grace wore a lace dress and carried a great bunch of daisies.
3. Lazy May lay in the shade.
4. Kate skated on the lake until quite late at night.
5. The Ladies' Aid Society had a cake sale in the rain.
6. Ray ate raisin bread and grape jam.
7. On Graduation Day there is a daisy chain at Vassar.
8. Wait for me while I take the late paper to this lady.
9. If we wait until later, it may stop raining.
10. Have you played a game called "racing"?

Can you answer these questions?

1. In what state were you born?
2. Which states are called the New England States?
3. Can you name the Great Lakes?
4. How many snakes can you name?
5. What makes the waves in the sea?

There are additional sentences for practice in this sound on page 130.

aɪ is the second sound in "knight." It is a combination of the a as in "dance" and the ɪ as in "city." Be careful not to say the first sound as though it were the ɑː in "father." Keep the back of your tongue up a little for this sound. Stress the first sound more than you do the second sound, ɪ. Blend the two.

Say these words, listening for the sound of aɪ.

Group I	Group II
ice	inquire
child	reply
mighty	aisle
fine	quiet
nine	diary
tried	knife
silence	lighthouse
climb	rifle
pride	height

Repeat each of these phrases three times.

hide the child	bright lights	my mind
fine time	quiet ride	side by side
high tide	nine times	night flight

In these sentences find the words which contain the sound of
ā̆ĭ. *Then read the sentences aloud.*

1. Irene tried to hide beside the fireplace.
2. Silas climbed the tree into which his kite fell.
3. The guide asked Hiram what time it was.
4. The hunter took a knife and a rifle because he was frightened by the tiger.
5. Jim has new tires on his bicycle.
6. The chimes rang out clearly in the silent night.
7. Why do flyers fear to fly at night?
8. I like rice, don't you?
9. The side door is five feet wide.
10. The vine twined around the gateway.

Can you answer these questions?

1. How high is the tallest building you know?
2. Have you tried to swim under water?
3. How high can you jump?
4. How many players are there on a ball team?
5. What do the red traffic lights mean?

There are some more exercises on this sound on page 130.

oṱŭ is the first sound in "ocean." It is a combination of the oṱ as in "obey" and the ᴜ as in "football." Keep the lips round for this sound.

Say these words aloud, listening for the sound of oṱŭ.

Group I	Group II
bowl	crow
fold	blown
know	flow
loan	coach
sew	stroll
boat	invoke
slope	provoke
float	bestow
broke	quote
soak	pillow

Repeat each of these phrases three times.

old gold	go home	fold your coat
bold soldier	throw roses	closed road
no older	slow boat	grow cold

122

In these sentences find the words which contain the sound of oʊ. *Then read the sentences aloud.*

1. Joseph rowed the boat all the way home.
2. This wind will blow the roses down.
3. Mona found a gold piece in the road.
4. Would you like to go to Rome?
5. We saw some motion pictures of President Roosevelt.
6. The old man told the children stories of the House of Gold.
7. Put on your oldest clothes when you go camping.
8. Don't try to row a boat on the ocean.
9. Oatmeal is sold at the grocery store.
10. Fold the paper so that it will hold the rose safely.

Can you answer these questions?

1. Do you know the song called "Sweet and Low"?
2. How old is the United States?
3. Where do pineapples grow?
4. Who owns Canada?
5. Can you row a boat?

If you need more practice on this sound, turn to page 130.

aʊ is the second sound in "cowboy." It is a combination of aː as in "garden" and ʊ as in "football." Be careful not to say the first sound as though it were the sound of æ as in "apple." Do not emphasize the ʊ sound.

Say these words aloud, listening for the sound of aʊ.

Group I	Group II
how	amount
loud	hour
sound	tower
town	howl
out	flower
outside	gown
cloudy	ground
proud	brow
south	rouse
founder	fountain

Repeat each of these phrases three times.

down and out	frown down	cloudy and showers
around the grounds	proud founder	round house
our town	brown owl	loud shouts

124

In these sentences find the words which contain the sound of aŭ. Then read the sentences aloud.

1. How the baseball crowd howls!
2. Hear how that wind howls around our house!
3. The hound howled when he found the scent.
4. How loud can you shout?
5. Howard wound a stout cord around the package.
6. The fountain showered water on the flowers which grew around its base.
7. The clouds are moving toward the south.
8. The boughs of the apple trees were covered with flowers.
9. There were brown beads around the neck of Martha's gown.
10. The mountain tops were hidden by the clouds.

Can you answer these questions?

1. How many pounds are there in a ton?
2. Where is the White House?
3. Who founded Quebec?
4. How large is your town?
5. Have you ever seen a clown in a circus?

You will find more practice sentences on page 130.

ɔɪ is the first sound in "oil." It is a combination of the
sound of ɔ as in "automobile" and ɪ as in "city." Be sure
to sound the first sound well.

Say these words aloud, listening for the sound of ɔɪ.

Group I	*Group II*
soil	spoil
point	Troy
join	destroy
oyster	joyous
noise	broil
voice	rejoice
loin	employ
embroider	royal
coil	boisterous
moisten	coined

Repeat each of these phrases three times.

moist soil	spoiled oysters	enjoy your voyage
joyous noise	poisoned points	those noisy toys
boys' voices	boiled in oil	royal coins

126

In these sentences find the words which contain the sound of
ɔɪ. *Then read the sentences aloud.*

1. The boys all joined in making a noise.
2. The farmer employed several men to keep the soil moist.
3. Some people think oil spoils salad dressing.
4. The oil burner is very noisy.
5. Gertrude found a pearl in her oyster.
6. Learn to join in the joys of others.
7. Roy spoiled his sister's embroidery.
8. When the royal carriage appeared, the loyal subjects cried, "Viva," in loud voices.
9. Avoid boisterous laughter or noisy voices.
10. Joyce was loitering in the hall waiting for Floyd to join her.

Can you answer these questions?

1. If you had a choice, which would you prefer, oysters or clams?
2. Where is oil found in the United States?
3. Can you name three American coins?
4. Can you point to the north, east, south, and west?
5. When did your state join the Union?

Practice these pairs of words.

earl	oil	furl	foil
curl	coil	verse	voice
journey	joining	learn	loin

Four of the diphthongs are made by adding the neutral mid-vowel "ə" as in "abroad" to ɪ, ɛ, ʊ, ɔ.

ɪə combines the ɪ as in "city" with ə as in "abroad."

Here are some words that contain the sound.

here, fears, weary, queer, clear
Here is the place where the deer cleared the wall.

ɛə combines ɛ as in "airplane" with ə as in "abroad."

Here are some words that contain the sound.

wear, air, heir, fairy, dare
There is the place where the bear was found.

ʊə combines ʊ as in "football" with ə as in "abroad."

Here are some words that contain the sound.

sure, poor, cure, moor, sewer
Mud is a sure cure for a bee's sting.

128

ɔɚ combines ɔ as in "automobile" with ɚ as in "abroad."

Here are some words that contain the sound.

four, pour, ore, core, soar
Here are four more apple cores.

Arrange the following words in four lists according to the diphthongs which they contain.

pier, tore, Mary, fury, care, weary, tears
queer, more, fewer, score, bare

Review of the Diphthongs

eɪ, aɪ, oʊ, aʊ, ɔɪ, ɪɚ, ɛɚ, ʊɚ, ɔɚ,

Diphthongs are made of two vowel sounds blended together. In the diphthongs studied here, the first sound is always stressed while the second element is always *unstressed*.

1. Always drink Grade A milk.
2. Do you like to bathe when the waves are high?
3. How old are you?
4. Mother baked a cake and put chocolate icing on it.
5. The snake coiled around the white pole.
6. The ice was frozen so hard that the children could skate on it.
7. Do you like to count the cars on a freight train?
8. Nice children play without making too much noise.
9. Have you ever tried to row a boat?
10. When you earn a coin, do you save it or spend it?
11. Call out the names of the players in your game.
12. Let us join the ladies.
13. When you sing the next verse, let your voice ring out.
14. Face the light when you have your picture taken.
15. What is the latest style in outdoor coats for boys?
16. Boil the water and I will make some tea.
17. If you learn your lessons every day, you will find the examinations easy.
18. When you write a letter, do not leave out polite greetings.
19. Boys and girls are joyful when vacation time comes.
20. This cold weather makes me want to go South.

21. How many girls are wearing curls today?
22. This is such a nice day that I shall row my boat around the Point.
23. Down South the climate is very fine.
24. The boys were lying in the sun with great big hats over their eyes.
25. Ice cream and cake were served at the Eighth Grade party.
26. The boys in the first term class made a sailboat out of wood.
27. Every day a boat sails up the Hudson River to Albany.
28. On a fine day this sail makes a pleasant trip.
29. Let us take the boat at the pier near Cortlandt Street.
30. The band is playing gayly, the sun is shining brightly, and we are on our way.
31. Those tall cliffs on the west side of the river are the Palisades.
32. They are in the State of New Jersey.
33. Now we are coming to West Point. Young men are trained there to become officers in the United States Army.
34. Let us leave the boat and visit the parade ground.
35. There is a fine view of the river from this place.
36. The poor boy who came here for his health is the heir to a fortune.
37. Are you sure that you poured clear water on those plants?
38. Would you care to see four bear cubs?
39. More and more queer buildings are being built.
40. Here is the door through which four kings have passed.

Special Drill on Sounds Frequently Mispronounced

ɑ

ɑ is often pronounced as æ or ǣ or even ɛ̃ə. It is not ǣsk but ɑsk. It is not bɛəskɪᴦt but bɑskɪt. Some people prefer to say bɑ·skɪt rather than bɑskɪt. Either is good American usage. Many Americans say bæskɪt. In words where the ɑ is followed by "st" as in "last," or "sk" as in "ask," or "nce" as in "dance," it is better to make the nice distinction of using the ɑ rather than the æ sound. Under no circumstances should the sound be flattened to ɛə or nasalized to ǣ. It is easier to get a good tone on ɑ than on æ in these words. This may be an added reason for preferring the broader sound. Be sure, however, not to say hɑnd for "hand" and mɑn for "man."

ɜɪ

There are two common mispronunciations of this sound. One is found among careless speakers in New York City. It makes a diphthong of the sound and rounds the lips for the first part of the diphthong. So "bird" becomes bʌɪd instead of bɜɪd, and "learn" becomes lɜɪən instead of lɜɪn.

Say these words aloud, taking special care of the ɜɪ sound.

   verse, third, first, thirty, thirsty, turn, girl

Be sure not to round the lips for this sound. Keep them in the neutral position. The second mispronunciation of ɜɪ is more common in the middle and far western parts of the country. This consists in turning the tip of the tongue back toward the throat for this sound. The correct position for

132

the tongue tip is low in the front of the mouth, behind the lower front teeth. Place it there and raise the middle of the tongue toward the roof of the mouth. Relax the lips. Make a voiced sound.

Try these words: journey, furnish, term, German

ʊ

ʊ, as in "football," is a rounded sound. Be sure to keep the lips well pursed for it. Read these words with special attention to lip rounding:

> good, cook, book, look, took, nook, put, could, would, wood

ɒ

ɒ as in "golf" is frequently mispronounced by unrounding the lips and prolonging the sound. Some American speakers use the short form of ɑ for this sound. Many others round the lips a little and make the sound halfway between the ɔː in "automobile" and ɑː in "garden." This tendency seems to be growing. On no account should the sound be lengthened to ɑː. Read these words aloud, using first ɑˑ then ɒ. Be sure not to use ɔː or ɑː.

> knowledge, cottage, folly, dot, doll, frolic, longer, Tom, coffee, hot

aɪ

aɪ, as in "ice," is frequently mispronounced by substituting ɑː, as in "garden," for the first element in the diphthong, a. Notice that for the right sound, a, you raise the back of the tongue a little and say the sound farther forward in the mouth than for the sound of ɑː. Practice saying it slowly until you can make the aɪ sound correctly. Practice these words aloud with special attention to the aɪ sound.

> night, nine, Friday, mind, line, tide, climb, grimy, brine, crime

aʊ

aʊ, as in "out." The difficulty here is just the opposite from that in the diphthong aɪ. Here the first element *should be* ɑː as in "garden." It is frequently mispronounced by substituting the a as in "ask" or even the nasalized æ as in "man." Read these words aloud, being sure to pronounce the first sound of the diphthong as ɑ.

> coward, frown, about, around, town, brow, loud, crouch, sound, ground

ɔɪ

ɔɪ, as in "oil," is frequently mispronounced by substituting the sound ɜː, as in "world," for the sound of ɔː, as in "automobile," in the first element in the diphthong. Practice these words with special emphasis on the first sound, ɔː.

> oyster, joint, coin, voice, coil, royal, boil, voyage, loiter, poison

Special Caution: Do not stress the second element ɪ or the word will become ɔːjəl instead of ɔɪl.

t and d

t and d are sometimes mispronounced by having them made on the teeth instead of on the gum *behind* the teeth. Do this exercise very carefully. Place the tip of the tongue lightly behind the upper teeth and say n-n-n-n-n-n-n-n.

Do you feel the spot where the tongue touches? You are not touching the back of the upper teeth, are you? Now touch the tip of the tongue to that same spot behind the upper front teeth and very lightly blow down a voiced sound for d. Do not *press* with the tongue. Read these words very carefully, feeling the tongue touch *behind* the teeth on the gum ridge.

> tied, diet, night, twine, dead, tight, teeth, third, dread, tent

s and z

All the sibilant sounds are difficult to produce well. For s and z, the important factors are: 1. The teeth should be very close together. 2. The sides of the tongue should be raised, touching the sides of the teeth. 3. The tongue tip should be raised toward the roof of the mouth and it should not touch anything. Read these words, taking particular care of the s and z sounds.

> sails, zinc, seas, spade, saves, string, asking, these, seethe, zenith

ʃ and ʒ

ʃ and ʒ are like s and z except that the tongue is more relaxed and the groove through the middle is shallower and broader. Try these pairs of words to prove this:

> save, shave; sewer, sure; buzz, bush; fasten, fashion

k

Be careful not to omit the k sound in words like these: section, accessory.

Try these pairs of words: session, section; assess, access

For special practice on the four sounds of ng, *see page 74.*

135

 juː

In some words the letter "u" or the combination "ew" is pronounced as though it were two sounds — j as in "yet" and uː as in "too." Such words are "usual" and "few." Here are some words which are mispronounced because the "j" is omitted. Say them aloud, being careful to pronounce the j sound:

Tuesday, newspaper, tune, suit, tulip, costume, avenue, knew, neutral, duty

Note: When the "u" or "ew" follows "l," the single sound uː is usually given: blue, *not* bljuː *but* bluː.

l and ɹ

Some people find difficulty in saying the sounds of "r" and "l." They sometimes say a "w" instead, so that "red" becomes "wed" and "lady" becomes "wady." If you find these sounds troublesome, practice raising the tongue to the roof of your mouth just behind your front teeth. Flatten it out so that the under side fits the shape of the front teeth. This is the position for "l." Make a voiced sound while holding the tongue up against the teeth. Now let the tongue drop for the vowel "ah." Try this again and again: l—ah, l—ah, lah, lah, lah.

Here are some words to practice:

lark, lady, lazy, lily, play, flag, glad, class, slide, blade

For the sound of "r," take the position for "l," then curl the tongue tip farther back without rounding the lips. Say aloud:

read, write, rang, roof, very, hurry, trunk, frown

136

Shibboleths

How do *You* say:—

help, self, handle
two, new, rule

man athletics
measure aviator
mine branch
ninety champion
now Chicago
oral Colorado
picture costume
police exquisite
question formidable
single gentleman
story government
thirty history
thought ignominy
three length
twenty library
twenty-five literature
water manger
with mingling
width museum

Group I

about
acts
any
asks
arrow
avenue
because
been
bread
breadth
candy
city
coffee
drawing
English
escapes
fifth
finger
first
five cents
glory
hundred
ice cream
idea
joins
laugh
lemonade
little

Group II

accessory
activity
address
adjoin
adjourn
adult
apparatus
Arkansas

oil-burner
personality
radiator
recognize
respects
romance
St. Louis
society
strength
comfortable

137

Phonetic Aids

Those who are familiar with the international phonetic symbols and who wish to do more advanced work, will find many valuable suggestions and aids in this section.

Production of the Consonants

p — is the first sound in "puppy." Press your lips lightly together. Now blow them apart with your breath. There are two ways of saying this sound. You can find more about that on page 148.

b — Press your lips together as you did in saying p, but this time blow them apart with a voiced sound.

m — Close your lips and make a voiced sound through your nose.

ᴍ — Push out your lips and make a small circle. Now blow through the little opening.

w — Push out your lips as you did for ᴍ. Blow a voiced sound through the small opening.

f — Bite your lower lip lightly with your upper teeth and blow out.

v — Bite your lower lip with your upper teeth as for f, but make a voiced sound.

θ — Press the tip of your tongue against the edge of your upper front teeth and blow out.

đ — Press the tip of your tongue against your upper teeth as you did for θ, but this time make a voiced sound.

t — Touch the tip of your tongue to the roof of your mouth just behind your upper front teeth. Now blow the tongue down quickly with the breath. *Caution:* Be careful not to press too hard with the tip of the tongue. Do not let the tongue touch the teeth. See page 148 for two ways of saying this sound.

d — Touch the tongue tip to the roof of your mouth as you did for t, but now blow it down with a voiced breath. *Caution:* Be sure you do not let the tongue tip touch the teeth.

n — Put the tip of the tongue on the roof of your mouth just as you did for t and d. Hold it there while you make a voiced sound through your nose. Look on page 151 for two ways of saying this sound.

l — Raise the front of your tongue to the roof of your mouth so that the under part touches your upper front teeth. Spread it until the sides of the tongue touch the side teeth. Make a voiced sound over the sides of the tongue. Be sure not to bunch the tongue for l. You can find two ways of saying l on page 151.

ɹ — Raise the tongue tip toward the roof of your mouth as you did for l. Then instead of touching the teeth and the roof of your mouth, just curl the tongue tip back toward your throat. Make a voiced sound.

s — Bring your teeth close together until they almost meet. Raise the tongue tip toward the roof of your mouth as though you were going to say t. Then send a small stream of air straight out between your front teeth. *Caution:* Do not let your tongue tip touch your front teeth. Be sure the sound comes through the front teeth.

z — Place the teeth in the same position as for s. Raise the tongue tip and send a voiced sound through the front teeth.

ʃ — Say s again. Then flatten the sides of the tongue so that the groove down the center is not so narrow. Now send the breath straight out between the front teeth. ʃ is not so sharp a sound as s.

ʒ — Make this sound just as you did ʃ, but send out a voiced sound.

tʃ — Raise the tip of the tongue as though you were going to say t. Then go rapidly into the sound of ʃ, as in "ships."

dʒ — Raise the tongue as though you were going to say d. Then go rapidly into the sound of ʒ, as in "treasure."

j — Raise the middle of your tongue toward the roof of your mouth and knock it down with a voiced breath.

k — Raise the back of your tongue to your soft palate. Then blow it down with the breath. If you have forgotten where the soft palate is, look at page 5. There are two ways of saying this sound. You can find out more about this on page 148.

g — Raise the back of your tongue as for k. Blow it down with a voiced breath.

ŋ — Raise the back of the tongue as for k and g. Hold it against the soft palate while you make a voiced sound through your nose. *Caution:* Be careful not to let the tongue fall until you have stopped making the voiced sound. There are four different pronunciations for the letters ng. You can find out more about them on page 74.

h — Just open your mouth and sigh.

141

Production of the Vowels

All vowels are voiced sounds.

iː — is the first sound in "eagle." Spread your lips in a smile and raise the front of your tongue toward the roof of your mouth.

ɪ — is the second sound in "city." It is a high front vowel. Put your tongue in the position for iː but do not let it stiffen.

eɪ — is the first sound in "elephant." Put your tongue in the position for ɪ, then lower it a little bit. Be careful not to lower the tongue too much. Keep the tip of the tongue lightly pressed against the back of the lower front teeth.

ɛɪ — is the first sound in "airplane." Place the tongue in the position for eɪ and then lower it slightly.

æ — is the first sound in "apple." Open your mouth a little more than you did for ɛɪ. Be sure to let the sound come through your mouth rather than through your nose.

a — is the second sound in "dance." This is the lowest of the front vowels. Open your mouth a little more than you did for æ. *Caution:* Be sure to keep the back of your tongue slightly raised so that the sound is farther forward than the ɑː in "garden."

ɜː — is the second sound in "world." Raise the middle of your tongue toward the roof of your mouth. Touch the tip lightly to the back of your lower front teeth. Let your lips hang naturally; do not round them.

142

ə — is the first sound in "abroad." It is used in unstressed syllables only. If you do not know what unstressed syllables are, you can find out on page 152. Place the tongue as for ɜː but let all the energy go out of it.

ʌ — is the first sound in "umbrella." It is the lowest middle vowel. It has nearly the same sound as ə but ʌ is used generally in a stressed syllable while ə is used always in unstressed syllables. Be careful not to make this sound too far back in your throat.

uː — is the second sound in "tools." It is the highest back vowel. Round your lips until they make a small circle. Now raise the back of your tongue and make a voiced sound.

ʊ — is the second sound in "football." It is made with the tongue and lips in the same position for uː, but the tongue is not so energized. Be sure to keep your lips rounded.

oʊ — is usually a diphthong and you will find it described among the diphthongs. However, when oʊ is in an unstressed syllable, or when it is followed by an unstressed syllable, it may be a pure vowel. Say the words "obey" and "going" aloud. Now say the word "old." You will notice that in "old" there are two sounds before you say the sound l, but in "obey" and in "going" there is only one sound. In these last words oʊ is a pure vowel.

ɔː — is the first sound in "automobile." Round your lips and then pull them down until they make a long opening.

143

ɒ — is the second sound in "golf." Round your lips as you did for ɔː but do not pull them down into such a long mouth. *Note:* Sometimes it helps if you put your mouth in the position for ɔː and then say ɑː as in "garden." Be sure to keep the lips slightly rounded.

ɑː — is the lowest back vowel. Allow your mouth to fall open and your tongue to lie flat in your mouth. *Note:* This is the sound the doctor asks you to make when he wants to look down your throat, because when you say ɑː your throat is wide open and your tongue is flat.

Length of Vowel Sounds

I. The vowel sounds in the following words are always
short:

knit	ɪ	put	ʊ
met	eт	not	ɒ
mat	æ	above	ə, ʌ

II. The vowel sounds in these words are long when they
are followed by a voiced sound. They are half-long
when they are followed by a voiceless consonant. Compare the following words:

seen	iː	seat	iˈ
there	ɛː	therefore	ɛˈ
word	ɜː	work	ɜˈ
rule	uː	root	uˈ
pause	ɔː	report	ɔˈ
hard	ɑː	heart	ɑˈ

If you know music, it may help you to think of these
three lengths in terms of note values.

iː as in "seen" = ♩ = 2 beats

iˈ as in "seat" = ♩. = 1½ beats

ɪ as in "sit" = ♪ = 1 beat

III. The sound a as in ask is always half-long.

*Note: The two dots following a symbol indicate that the
sound is long. One dot means that it is half-long.
If there is no dot, the sound is short.*

IV. Divide this list of words into three groups. In Group 1 place all those with long vowels; in Group 2 place all those with half-long vowels; in Group 3 place all those with short vowels.

heat	wear	path	bird
bit	rule	arm	burn
wet	roof	art	first
cup	good	head	pool
salt	dog	bead	farm

Rules for Lengthening Consonants

We lengthen a consonant after a short vowel in a stressed syllable when it occurs before a pause.

Here are some examples of long consonants.

> his   hɪzː
> met   mɛtː
> rap   ɹæpː

Compare them with these short consonants.

> pools   pʰuːlz
> curb   kʰɜːb
> halt   hɔːlt
> harp   hɑˑp

l, m, n, ŋ are lengthened when they come before another voiced consonant in the same stressed syllable

> called   kʰɔːlɪd
> dreamed   dɹiːmɪd
> crowned   kɹɑˈʊˑnɪd
> belonged   bɪlɒŋɪd

147

Two Ways of Saying p, t, k

When p, t, or k are followed by a vowel or a diphthong, or when they are followed by a pause, they are puffed out quite strongly. This is called the aspirated form. It is marked in phonetic script like this: pʰ, tʰ, kʰ. It occurs in such words as:

peep	pʰiˌpʰ
tight	tʰaɪtʰ
cook	kʰʊkʰ

When p, t, k, are followed by a consonant, they are not puffed out so strongly. This is called the unaspirated form. It is marked in phonetic script like this: pᵢ, tᵢ, kᵢ.

It occurs in such words as:

play	pˌleɪˀ
try	tˌɹaɪ
crow	kˌɹoʊʊ̆

Say these pairs of words and see whether you can hear the difference between the aspirated and the unaspirated forms.

pray	pay	track	tack	cow	crow
pry	pie	try	tie	crave	cave
plump	pump	truck	tuck	creep	keep

Notice that in some of these words there are both aspirated and unaspirated consonants. Do not forget that final p, t, k before a pause are always aspirated. "Act" is neither ækˌ nor ækʰtʰ but ækˌtʰ.

148

Syllabication

When a word has more than one vowel or diphthong in it we break it up into parts so that we can say it more easily. Each of these parts is called a syllable. In the word "mother" there are two syllables, "mo-ther." In phonetics we should write the word *mother* this way: mʌ ðə and we should show the syllables by leaving a space between them. Sometimes in writing phonetics we also draw a line under each syllable like this:

m ʌ ð ə

When we divide a word into syllables, we have usually a vowel or a diphthong in each syllable.[1] Then we place at the beginning of each syllable as many consonant sounds as we can say easily, like this:

| mo ther | twen ty | rich ly |
| sing ing | ques tion | re strain |

You will notice that the "ng" in the first syllable of "singing" is attached to the first syllable because no English word begins with "ng." But we put "str" on the second syllable of "restrain" because we often have that combination of sounds at the beginning of English words, such as "street" and "straight."

Now divide the following words into syllables. If you are not sure, say them aloud. Be careful to have a vowel

[1] See p. 151 for three exceptions to this rule.

149

sound in each syllable and to put as many consonant sounds at the beginning of a syllable as you would find at the beginning of an English word. Notice that in the words "reply" and "restrict" all the consonants which follow the first vowel are placed at the beginning of the second syllable because we have English words which begin with "pl" and "str"—so it is "re ply" and "re strict." But it is "im press" and "in vite." Why?

How many of these words can you divide correctly? If you are in doubt re-read the rules:

fancy	polite	safety	begin	leaves
about	front	city	barked	wonder
under	blazing	magic	drinking	boxes
united	bookworm	insist	dances	saucer
snowball	aster	gateway	sidewalk	lettuce

Syllabic Consonants

Sometimes when l, n, or m come at the end of a word, they form a syllable all by themselves.   Like this:

garden   gɑːdn̩

little   lɪtl̩

prism   pɹɪzm̩

This "syllabic" consonant is marked this way in phonetics: a small vertical line is placed *under* the symbol—l̩, n̩, m̩,

Such words are written like this:

seʈvn̩,   bætl̩,   fæʃn̩

Notice that in a word like "battle," the syllabic l makes the t an unaspirated sound.   If you have forgotten what that means, look on page 148.

Stress

In music you have learned about the heavy beat and the light beat. In saying English words we have some syllables which have the strong beat and others which have a light one. Like this:

In the word "candy," "can" has the strong beat, while "dy" is just whispered. In the word "family," "fa" gets the strong beat, while "i" and "ly" get only a light beat. This heavy beat we call stress and the syllable which gets the heavy beat we call the stressed syllable while the ones which get the light beat we call the unstressed syllables.

In the word "family" "fa" is the stressed syllable, while "i" and "ly" are unstressed. Which are the stressed and which the unstressed syllables in "candy," "baby," "grandma," "laughing," "forget," "begin," "syllable"?

We mark the stressed syllable like this '. In many of the dictionaries this mark comes after the stressed syllable, but in writing in phonetics it is placed BEFORE the syllable, so that you may know that the syllable is stressed before you begin to say it.

Like this: ˈfæ mɪ lɪr

Rewrite these words, putting the stress marks before the stressed syllable.

market	matches	patchwork
banana	practice	composition
fancy	penny	reader
bandage	paper	arithmetic
basket	shepherd	spelling
collar	blinded	fractions
beauty		syllable

152

Strong and Weak Forms

Say aloud the sentence, "The boy eats a piece of bread." What words do you stress as you say it?

Why do the words *boy, eats, piece, bread* get more stress than *the* and *a*?

It is because the stressed words carry the message, while the unstressed ones are not so important. In order, then, that we shall know that the words which carry the message are more important than the others, we make the unimportant words a little less noticeable. We "weaken" these connecting words. Very often this is done by saying the vowel ə instead of the regular vowel in these unimportant words. Sometimes the whole word is contracted and some sounds are left out. Like this: *I've* for *I have*.

"The" spells ðiː when we say it alone. That is its *strong* form. But when we put it in a sentence, then we weaken it to ðə or ðɪ. So that in the sentence, "The boy eats a piece of bread," we should weaken ðiː to ðɪ and eɪ to ə. This is what we say: ðɪ bɔɪ ɪˈts ə piˈs əv bɹeɪd.

We often say *I've* for *I have*, and *I'd* for *I had*. Many short, unimportant words have these two forms. When we say them alone, they have the strong form; but when we say them in sentences, they are weakened. Here are some examples of strong and weak forms:

	STRONG FORM	WEAK FORM
it is	ɪt ɪz	ɪtˌs
of	ɒv	əv
that	ðæt	ðət
them	ðeɪm	ðəm

153

	STRONG FORM	WEAK FORM
I have	aɪ hæv	aɪv
we shall	wiː ʃæl	wiˑl
the	ðiː	ðə or ðɪ
cannot	kʰænɒt	kant
and	ænd	nd or ənd

Here are some sentences using these weak forms. Be careful to read them correctly.

I have taken a slice of cake.
Here is a book.
Let us sit down.
We shall have rain in the morning.
I can't read this line.
Bread and butter are good to eat.

Note: Before a vowel, "the" is weakened to ðɪ rather than to ðə.

Do not be afraid to use weak forms. They will make your speech flow freely. But be sure not to think that using weak forms is an excuse for speaking carelessly. It is not right to say n for *and,* nor fæk for *fact,* nor kʰʌmɪn for *coming.* But do not say, "I saw *a* boy eating *a* piece *of* cake." Be particularly careful to use the right weak forms in reading aloud. You should use them just as you do for speaking.

154

Intonation

Every language has its own tune. Say this sentence out loud, "I like dogs." Notice that the words go down the hill like this:

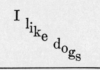

Say this sentence, "There goes John." Those words go down hill, too, like this:

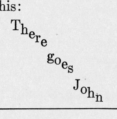

If you were to draw a picture of the way the words go down hill, it would look like this:

I like dogs.　　　　　There goes John.

You will see that there is a big sweep or curve down on the words "dogs" and "John." That is the regular tune of English. Sometimes we hear a person speaking who comes from another country. Even when he pronounces all the English words just as we do, sometimes he says them to a different tune and it doesn't sound quite like English.

When you tell a story about anything and make a statement such as the two sentences, "I like dogs" and "There goes John" the words all go down hill and the last word has a long curve down.

When we draw a picture of this, we use a line to measure from, so we call this the measuring line. _____

Every stressed syllable is marked with a heavy dot like this __•__

Every unstressed syllable is marked with a light dot, like this __·__

Every syllable that slides down hill is marked this way
—ϡ—

Every syllable that slides up hill is marked this way
__✓__

Now we are ready to study the two tunes which are most often used in English.

Rule I. When we make a complete statement or tell a whole story, such as the ones in the sentences, "I like dogs," and "There goes John," each of the words has one stressed syllable, and they all slide down hill. On the last word in each sentence—"dogs" and "John"—there is a big sweep or glide. This is very important.

156

Read these sentences, watching for the big glide at the end:

Dogs often bark _____,

Cows give milk _____,

This is the first day of May _____,

(Notice that the highest sound is the first *stressed* syllable.)

Rule II.   Whenever the statement is not complete, the last stressed syllable glides up.

When the princess opened her eyes _____

As Mary was walking to school _____

When a question can be answered by "yes" or "no", the last stressed syllable glides up too.

Are you going to school? _____ Yes _____,

Rule III.   When a question begins with a question word like "what," "where," "when," "why," the tune is the same as in Rule I and the words slide down.

Where are you going? _____, I am going home. _____,

157

Students who speak or hear more than one language often use the intonation pattern of one language with the words of the other.   Here are some other intonation patterns—

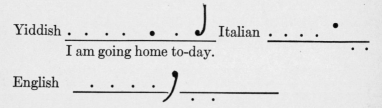

Yiddish . . . . . . •   Italian . . . . •

I am going home to-day.

English   . . . . .

If your voice goes up in the wrong place, practice reading these phrases with a strong downward curve:

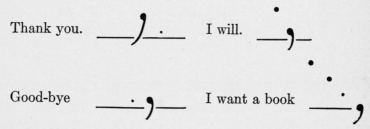

Thank you.   _____ .   I will.

Good-bye   . _____   I want a book

Now say these sentences aloud and then draw a picture of how they sound.   If you are not sure, read over the rules and then see which rule is used for that sentence.

1. This is June.
2. I like to skate.
3. Are you going to school?
4. Where is Jane?
5. I found a mushroom.
6. This is my seat.
7. My dog's name is Jack.
8. How old are you?
9. Have you any money?
10. There is Jenny's ring.
11. When does school close?
12. Here is the hat that I found.
13. Can you read that sign?
14. Please give me more bread.

Grouping

Although, when we practice speech exercises, we often work on single words, when we speak to each other, we usually speak in groups of words.

We/ do/ not/ speak/ like/ this/—We speak/ like this/

These groups of words, which are bound together when we speak, we call phrases. They usually have in them one stressed syllable and all the unstressed syllables which would naturally go with it. Like this:

> Every afternoon / I go home.
> the break of day/
> good bye/
> come again/

In phonetic script we write a phrase like this.

$$kʌm \quad ə'geɪn |$$

The single bar marks the end of the phrase. When we wish to pause for breath at the end of a phrase, we mark that with a double bar like this: ‖

$$ðə \quad 'bɹeɪk | əv \quad 'deɪ ‖$$

Mark the phrases in these sentences.

1. Come here and get your candy.
2. The sun is shining.
3. This is the house that Jack built.
4. Tomorrow is my birthday.

Ear Training Exercises

1—Match the following words according to vowel sounds.

bear	wood	learn	wheat
knee	fern	hair	should

2—Match these words according to whether the first sound is voiced or voiceless. *Caution:* The *sounds* and not the *spelling* are to be matched.

tight	throw	ink	pack	dismiss
order	labor	felt	engage	setting
brain	axes	hill	cherry	gorilla

3—Now divide the words in Exercise 2 according to whether the *last* sound is voiced or voiceless.

4—Separate these words into three columns according to whether the sounds represented by the underlined letters in each are: (1) vowels, (2) consonants, (3) diphthongs.

large	pound	end	lunch	violet
young	beach	cook	banana	fright
leave	grasp	water	trunk	leather

5—Can you indicate in phonetic script the pronunciation of the sounds underlined in Exercise 4?

6—Can you arrange these consonants in groups under these headings?

a—lip sounds
b—lip and teeth sounds
c—lip and tongue sounds
d—tip of the tongue sounds

e—back of the tongue sounds
f—middle of tongue sounds
g—nasal sounds

k, g, j, s, t, d, l, ɹ, ŋ, z, ʃ, θ, ḍ, v, f, w, b, m, p, ʍ, ʒ

7—Can you group these vowels as front, middle, or back?

uː ʊ ɔт iː ɜː ə æ ɑ
ɒ ʌ ɔː ɛː e ɑː ɪ

8—Can you arrange these sounds as consonants, vowels, and diphthongs?

ɪə a ɛə ɔт aʊ θ ŋ ʊ aɪ
ɔɪ ɔə eɪ ɜː ɪ ḍ

9—Can you write these words in phonetic script?

boy	freeze	they	pier
cow	word	choose	sure
long	rough	fault	four
sat	mesh	garage	yes
thin	where	push	hedge

10—Write these sentences in phonetic script.

1. Shut the door.
2. Erase the blackboard.
3. Pass me the chalk.
4. Come to order.

5. Open the window.
6. Raise the shades.
7. Place the flowers in the bowl.
8. Take off your hat in the house.

161

Vowel Scale

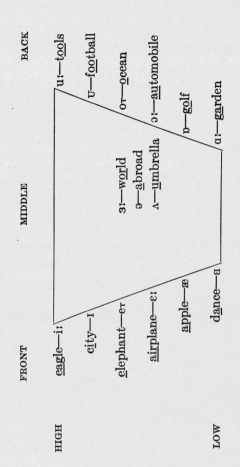

HIGH	FRONT	MIDDLE	BACK
	eagle—iː		uː—tools
	city—ɪ		ʊ—football
	elephant—eɪ	ɜː—world	oʊ—ocean
		ə—abroad	ɔː—automobile
	airplane—ɛə	ʌ—umbrella	
	apple—æ		ɒ—golf
LOW	dance—ɑ		ɑː—garden

Adapted from the vowel chart of Professor William Tilly.

Consonant Chart

VOICELESS	NASAL	VOICED
p—puppy ʍ—whale	*Lip Sounds* m—mail	b—baseball w—wind
f—fish	*Lip and Teeth Sounds*	v—violin
θ—theater	*Teeth and Tongue Sounds*	ð—feathers
t—tennis	*Tip of Tongue and Hard Palate Sounds* n—news	d—David
	Blade of Tongue Sounds	l—lion ɹ—railroad
s—stars ʃ—ships tʃ—chariot	*Sibilant Sounds*	z—zebra ʒ—treasure dʒ—jump
	Middle of the Tongue Sound	j—yesterday
k—kite	*Back of the Tongue and Soft Palate Sounds* ŋ—singing	g—gull
h—horse	*Aspirate Sound*	

163

The Sounds of English

CONSONANTS

Key Words	International Phonetic Alphabet (Printed)	International Phonetic Alphabet (Written)
puppy	p	
baseball	b	
mail	m	
whale	ʍ	
wind	w	
fish	f	
violin	v	
theater	θ	
feathers	ð	
tennis	t	
David	d	
news	n	
lion	l	
railroad	ɹ	
stars	s	
zebra	z	
ships	ʃ	
treasure	ʒ	
chariot	tʃ	
jump	dʒ	
yesterday	j	
kite	k	
gull	g	
singing	ŋ	
horses	h	